A Brick on the Head

Peter Waite

Matador
Unit E2 Airfield Business Park,
Harrison Road, Market Harborough,
Leicestershire. LE16 7UL
Tel: 0116 2792299
Email: books@troubador.co.uk
Web: www.troubador.co.uk/matador
Twitter: @matadorbooks

ISBN 978 1803132 754

British Library Cataloguing in Publication Data.
A catalogue record for this book is available from the British Library.

Printed and bound in the UK by TJ Books LTD, Padstow, Cornwall
Typeset in 11pt Minion Pro by Troubador Publishing Ltd, Leicester, UK

Matador is an imprint of Troubador Publishing Ltd

This book is dedicated to the people of Ukraine

Introduction

I belong to a very fortunate generation. Born in 1951, I just about escaped the hardship and rationing that spilled over from World War II and yet my parents and other adults I knew as I grew up had been through it and so I felt touched by it. Likewise, my grandparents had had even worse experiences in the 1914-1918 Great War. Both of my grandfathers survived war in the trenches to return to 'a land fit for heroes'. Like many such survivors they were reluctant to talk about their experiences but I was marked by some of their values, character and a kind of gallows humour that allowed them to cope with all that they had endured.

This is the story of a fully paid-up member of the 'Baby Boomer' generation. It is told almost entirely from memory so, whilst I have tried to be true to the facts, personalities and times, I must apologise in advance for any inaccuracies. Unfortunately I kept no diaries except for a few notebooks randomly and intermittently scribbled during my late teens and early twenties. Regrettably, I hardly discussed our family story with my parents when I had the chance and now they are both gone. My brother and sister have provided valuable information, as have my friends and I am grateful for all their help. I have always been a bit of a day-dreamer, a dabbler, a jack-of-all-trades and master of none and it was only when I began to write this story that I came to realise that, for many years, I enjoyed what is known as 'The Bachelor Lifestyle'. However, in case I give the impression that my life has been nothing but a joy-ride, I must stress that, in writing this book, I have largely skipped through the day-to-day slog of earning a living.

Setting down my story has been a satisfying and enjoyable exercise and, if there is one piece of advice that I would humbly offer it is, if your parents are still around, talk to them more, listen and learn. People of my era are products of the years immediately following World War Two; a period of austerity combined with the heady relief that finally the madness and bloodshed was over. Blessed with free education (including a little bottle of milk every day), free healthcare, no National Service and therefore no compulsion to fight anybody, mine was and is a truly fortunate generation. It now seems that few lessons have been learned and, once again, our world is faced with mindless slaughter in Europe and beyond.

One

Bomb-Site

I was born a Yellowbelly on the 12th of April 1951. Yes - a Yellowbelly. A native of Lincolnshire, that little-known and largely agricultural county, sprawling from the East Midlands to the east coast of England. The origins of the colourful title are unclear and there are many theories, but the most plausible is that the officers of the Royal North Lincolnshire Militia wore bright yellow waistcoats on the battlefield. As far as I know, the name has nothing to do with an attack of jaundice or with inherent cowardice. Let's face it, if you are stupid enough to go charging into battle wearing a yellow target of a waistcoat, you might be accused of many things; foolhardiness, idiocy, exhibitionism, bad dress sense – but you're certainly no coward.

It is said that life is a circle. We are born, it is assumed, with no memories; unable to walk or speak, dribbling and sleeping for much of each day with no responsibility for our actions. And, sadly, this is also how many of us will end our days. Anyhow, I came yelling and gurgling into this world in my grandparents' little house in Rectory Lane in the village of Waddington, a few miles south of Lincoln. I don't know why my mother gave birth in that place, but it might have had something to do with the fact that my parents lived in a home-made caravan on a bomb-site and maybe the birthing facilities there weren't quite up to scratch.

My parents were both Yellowbellies too. My dad, Les, like me born in Waddington and my mum, Betty, from Grimsby, a coastal town which, for much of the 20th century, hosted the world's largest fishing fleet. They were both of that generation still largely moulded by the Victorian era. There was strict discipline but also, especially in those rural surroundings, great freedom. This combination of strictness and freedom, I'm pleased to say, formed the framework for my own upbringing.

I was always intrigued by the stories my parents told me of their childhood. My father, born and bred in Waddington, rarely left the village when he was a boy. I believe that, when he was a little older, the church ran occasional charabanc outings to the seaside but, apart from those rare escapes, the village was his world. That does't mean that life was dull for him. In those days there were several farms within the village itself. I remember saying once to my grandad, 'I'll bet it was quiet in Waddington when you were a lad?'

'You must be joking', he said, 'What with the cows mooing, cocks crowing, dogs barking, steam-engines puffing and horses neighing, you couldn't hear yourself think!' As a small boy, one job my dad enjoyed was delivering the huge working carthorses to and from their pastures down Somerton Gate Lane (or Milking Hill, as we called it) for a well-earned rest. These gentle giants had to be ridden bare-back but the young village lads were hardly grown-up enough to straddle the horses' broad backs so they perched on as best they could, clinging to their manes for dear life, as they steered them to and from the lush pasture.

Village kids were expected to help with all kinds of farm work. Of course the main cereal harvest was very important and that is why long summer school holidays first came about. Village people, young and old, were all expected to help but, as well as cereals, lots of root crops had to be lifted. Lincolnshire is still famous for its potatoes and, in my father's time and right up to quite recently, all had to be picked by hand. It really is back-breaking work. The farmer made several passes with a rusty old contraption called a 'spinner', towed behind a little old grey 'Fergie' (Massey Ferguson) tractor. Wheezing its way along the rows, the machine brought the potatoes to the surface ready for gathering. Bent double for hours on end and paid only by actual weight in the baskets, we certainly knew when we'd spent a day 'tatie-pickin''.

The young children of the village had few toys so they had to innovate and adapt and use their imaginations to amuse themselves. The main Lincoln to Grantham road, now the A607, cuts through the eastern part of Waddington but, until the 1940s, much of it was little more than a glorified limestone farm track. When my dad was a boy, there was so little through-traffic that he and his friends used to play football there. Nobody could afford a proper leather ball, so they used an inflated pig's bladder. Parts of pigs were easy to come by in those days since almost all villagers kept a fat porker in the back yard – the equivalent of today's waste-disposal units and re-cycling centres. Plus, my Great Uncle Herbert was the village butcher so there was always a ready supply of bladders (and any other spare bits) for Dad to play with. Apparently, apart from a few traction engines and horse-drawn wagons, the only interruptions to the football matches were occasional coal lorries and the doctor's car.

There was however, around that time, a colourful character in Waddington called Yankee Gillyat who is well worth a mention. He was of great interest to the village boys because he used to ride around on a very early motor cycle wearing his peaked cap backwards so it wouldn't be blown off in a headwind. My dad and his pal Len Thomson were in awe of Yankee. Here is an excerpt from the notebook of Horace Dudley, village photographer 1890-1946.

April 11th 1909

This morning I photographed Yankee Gillyat with his daughter and motorcycle outside 'High House' in Rectory Lane. Apparently in 1861, Tom and Fred Gilyatt, two brothers, left Waddington to fight in the American Civil War and in fact were awarded land for reclamation. Tom returned with a mysterious Mexican wife and a baby son. Just as mysteriously as they had arrived, they left, leaving the baby to be brought up by old Jim Kelsey – The child was nicknamed 'Yankee' and it has stuck with him.

Yankee is a known poacher and along with Mr Skaith cooks rabbit in the back of Skaith's shop in the market place, probably drinking methylated spirit with the meat.

At the local farthing dances held in a tap room at the Horse and Jockey, he accompanies popular songs on his cherished fiddle. He wears his cap back to front and it's rumoured that he sleeps on a bed of gold sovereigns.

If the date is correct, when my dad was a young boy, this means that Yankee would by then have been in his sixties. I remember Dad telling me that he and his friend, Len Thompson, when they were only eleven or twelve years old, were allowed by Yankee to ride his motorcycle around the fields. He said it was a Harley-Davidson but I'm not sure about that.

Down in the valley below Waddington and the neighbouring village of Harmston flow two rivers, the Brant and the Witham, meeting at a place known by locals as Spike Island. Through the generations these rivers were of course great attractions for children of all ages, providing water-based entertainment for one and all. The Witham frequently burst its banks, flooding the surrounding fields. In the depths of winter the water-meadows often froze solid, creating immense ice rinks. Len Thompson somehow acquired skates and the boys goaded each other into performing ever more daring stunts, picking up grazes and bruises galore.

My dad always had an enquiring mind. He was eager to learn everything about anything and, as he grew older he was able to turn his hand to all kinds of practical skills. Later, as a father, he would like nothing better than sharing this knowledge with us children. Despite, or maybe because of, the confines of his simple village upbringing, he always had a tremendous sense of adventure. After his schooling, he worked at the little village bakery for J Cooper Lawson (at that time even very modest villages had bakers, a post office, cobblers, clock repairers, blacksmiths, carpenters/undertakers, butchers and so on) but very soon his life changed dramatically.

The Second World War took young lads like my dad from villages and towns up and down the land. He was recruited into the Coldstream Guards, as was his brother, Ronald and he was thus subsequently exposed to the horrors of warfare, the comradeship, hardship and adventure as they fought through Europe. What a change from simple village life. It's only when I consider how this must have affected him that I begin to understand the father that he became. Very tough, reserved - almost shy, resourceful, funny and clever. He rarely spoke of the horrors of that war but, when he did, it was moving and chilling at the same time.

My mum had worked in a Grimsby shoe shop in the early war years and she too had a brush with danger when a surprise bombing raid hit the street as she was on a bus heading home after work. Later she joined the Women's Land Army and lived and worked on farms providing much-needed wartime food. She met my dad at a village dance in Waddington Village Hall. Right next to the village is an important RAF station, RAF Waddington, which had opened in 1916 as a First World War training camp for the Royal Flying Corps. Waddington Heath, just to the east of the village, used to host popular horse-races before the land was requisitioned and the airfield was built.

The camp grew and was an important base for heavy bombers, including Lancasters, in the 1940s.

Later, during the Cold War, Waddington was home to the mighty Vulcan bombers, providing the UK's nuclear deterrent and it is still important today as a major intelligence gathering and Reaper drone control centre. To reach those village hall dances in the forties Mum had to cycle to Waddington so, rather than pedal several miles all the way round the secure perimeter, she took a short cut from Waddington Heath on a (now closed off) lane across the airfield. Of course she was caught, but the guards allowed a pretty young woman on her way. Interestingly, the airfield was also built right across the old Roman road known as Ermine Street, which was a major route for the legions marching from London to York via Lincoln.

My parents were married in the old stone church at Great Coates near Grimsby in January 1950. Somehow my dad had got hold of a set of American plans showing how to build a caravan and he immediately set about creating one to provide a new marital home. Built from aluminium on a timber framework, a little bit like early aircraft construction, when completed it provided a snug home for them and their new offspring, featuring fitted gas lighting and a coke-burning stove. During my early months in the caravan I slept in a wall-mounted folding bunk/cradle contraption supported by chains. The problem of where to site their new home was solved, surprisingly, by the village rector.

During the war the Luftwaffe had made several attempts to attack RAF Waddington. They weren't amused by the RAF sending bombers over Germany so, in the early hours of the 9th of May 1941, they decided to reciprocate by dropping bombs and a couple of aerial mines (parachute mines) to try to destroy the airfield. The bombs did destroy the NAAFI canteen, killing the manager, Mrs Constance Raven and ten or eleven other personnel on the base. Later the NAAFI opened a club named The Raven Club in her memory. One of the two parachute mines drifted off target and scored a direct hit on the 12th century village church of St Michael and All Saints, completely destroying it and causing further damage to several houses and the Horse & Jockey pub.

As well as the eleven people who were killed on the base in that raid, there was one victim in the village itself, namely Eva Hall, a girl living in a house close to the church. The church took most of the force of the blast and probably helped prevent much more bloodshed and damage. Thankfully, the RAF station continued to function as before, with Waddington playing an important part in the brutal struggle against Germany.

The upshot of all this was that, the area where the ancient church had once stood, was now a bomb-site, a piece of wasteland, which remained so until a new stone church was built and eventually consecrated in 1954. My dad received permission to park his newly-created caravan on the site until he could find a more permanent home for it – and so we began our very early months of life as a family in a home-built mobile shack sitting on a bomb-site.

Clearly this arrangement was not ideal so, when local farmer Ron Gambles of Green Farm, offered to let them site it in a spare corner of his farmyard, my parents jumped at the chance and the caravan was duly parked by a stand of ancient walnut trees close to the edge of Waddington Cliff. (Not an actual cliff but a section of the Lincoln Edge, a gentle limestone escarpment) with far-reaching views to the west over the Trent valley and wonderful pink sunsets.

Having become upwardly mobile, as it were, from bomb-site to farmyard, my parents now threw themselves into hard work and domestic bliss to further improve their fortunes. They had almost nothing, but I'm guessing that the rent they paid to Ron the farmer was almost nothing too. They also helped around the farm and shared in some of the produce and food that was available. The farm was of the traditional mixed variety, so we were surrounded by chickens, geese, ducks, guinea-foul, pigs and cattle as well as all the paraphernalia used for ploughing, harvesting and so on.

Mrs Gambles, the ever-jolly farmer's wife was always bustling around. She used to churn butter in her kitchen and was like a mother hen to us all. My mother used to tell me that, as a baby, I never stopped yelling – so much so that Farmer Ron named me ''Appy Arry'. Somewhere I have a crumpled black and white photo of me on the farm, as a toddler, holding our cat Tim, fully-stretched out and upside-down. I look very pleased with myself. The cat was just about as long as I was tall and he didn't seem to mind being dangled in such an undignified way.

Around this time my dad managed to get a job at a nearby iron foundry. He was over six feet tall, very fit and, like most people of that time, never carried any excess weight but it soon became apparent that working at the foundry was very bad for his health. The money was good in a time of austerity and it was certainly badly needed to support a growing family. My sister Susan had been born in December 1952. Dad had lost loads of weight, was now painfully thin and began to cough up soot – so he decided that he would have to make a change.

For a while he worked at Hindle's, a small engineering company in Lincoln, where he learned welding and metal-working skills. But, ever since leaving the army, he had wanted to start a business so now was his chance. He teamed up with a like-minded man, Ray Blades, who had left the RAF and also wanted to work for himself. They clubbed together and bought two wrecked-up ex-army trucks for a pittance and spent all their waking time building one serviceable lorry which they sprayed pea-green. The foundry would probably have killed my dad if he had continued there, whereas now he and Ray were masters of their own destiny. Things weren't easy for them. They couldn't afford new tyres so were continually picking up punctures. Breakdowns were frequent but, by sheer hard work and determination, they slowly but surely built up a worthwhile business.

The fledgling enterprise was given a bitter-sweet helping hand in 1953. At the end of January that year a tremendous 'storm tide' hit the North Sea, primarily affecting the coasts of Great Britain, The Netherlands and Belgium. A lethal combination of very high spring tides and gale-force winds overwhelmed sea defences all around the North Sea. In Lincolnshire alone the terrible floods caused more than 300 deaths and 30,000 people were forced from their homes. In desperation, every possible resource was called upon to help and the local authorities summoned diggers, trucks, pumps and all manner of equipment in an attempt to mend breaches in the sea defences as quickly as possible.

In Waddington there was a limestone quarry owned by a semi-recluse called 'Old Mark' Howden. Dad had befriended him as a boy and, when he and Ray started their truck business, they had agreed a price with Old Mark to extract stone. Stone that was not good enough for building was crushed into hardcore. Initially, they smashed the stone with sledgehammers but later they mounted an old engine on a chassis coupled with a grinding contraption, simply known as 'The Crusher'. With the name and temperament of an all-in wrestler, it digested lumps of stone fed in by hand and clanking, smoking and shuddering, it spat out the rock as hardcore. This was then loaded onto their trucks (by now they had two of them) by shovel and driven thirty-odd miles to the coast to be used in rebuilding the sea defences. At this time Dad and Ray would be shovelling and driving flat-out from dawn to nightfall. It was back-breaking work and, when they weren't actually loading and driving, they were working long into the night carrying out repairs and maintenance on the trucks.

Memory plays strange hazy tricks and I used to think I remembered being in a pram. Unlikely. However, the very first memory I am certain of was a sharp and painful shock indeed. I was about three years old and, by that age, I went almost everywhere with my father. He would be driving his old beaten-up green Bedford truck and I would be his passenger, clinging on tight as we bounced and clattered our way down rough farm tracks and country roads. On Brant Road, in the valley right below Waddington, there used to be a brick works owned by the Lincoln Brick Company. Dad had a contract collecting and delivering bricks and I used to love going there with him. The trucks were loaded by hand and, on this particular occasion, he was collecting reject bricks that could simply be thrown onto the truck. Dad was being helped by a rough and ready labourer called Brian Lockwood, who was obsessed by Western comics and seemed to imagine he was some kind of cowboy hero.

The men were happily chucking bricks into the truck, laughing and joking as usual. Meanwhile, I had clambered out and the nice man from the brickworks was offering me a sweet from a little paper bag. Just as I raised the sweetie to my mouth, a brick sailed gracefully over the truck and landed right on top of my young head. Needless to say I screamed and I cried and I howled and I bled and I bled ... a lot. My poor father charged round the truck to find me flat-out. He must have thought I'd been killed but, whether I'd inherited a good thick skull or whether the blow was at a lucky angle, I don't know. Anyway I survived to tell the tale.

I remember being in the truck again and it being driven at screaming pitch up Waddington Hill to the doctor's surgery. Miraculously, my little skull was not fractured but stitches were stitched, antiseptics were dabbed, jabs were jabbed in my bottom and I was whole again. Believe me, even though I was only three years old, it sticks in the memory. Incidentally, it didn't stop me enjoying riding in the lorry with my dad..and it certainly didn't put me off sweets!

Two

Brutus and the Barn

Dad and Ray were by now making a good living by sheer hard work and they began to expand the business slowly but surely. They had been renting space in Farrier's Yard in Waddington High Street. This was one of the old disused farms within the village, fronted by a crumbling stone cottage. Times were changing for farmers and the writing was on the wall for village farms in particular, which were little more than smallholdings. Farrier's Yard was flanked on the south side by another such farm, then still in use, owned by Walt Black and on the north side by yet another owned by George Harley. There was an open cart shed – ideal for parking lorries and machinery and a small barn which served as a workshop. They had saved money and were now in a position to buy the yard. This must have been an exciting turning-point for my parents as well as for Ray and his new wife Brenda, who worked in the village post office.

Mum and Dad wasted no time in moving the caravan into the new property. Immediately behind the main yard was a small raised area with a couple of apple trees in a vegetable plot of rich dark soil and, behind that, a small paddock. They built a ramp of hardcore up to the raised area and the paddock and formed a base for the caravan just in front of the vegetable plot. A shed was installed to one side of the site to serve as a small office for the growing business, which was now expanding into hiring out plant and machinery to local builders, farmers and the like.

Life in our small caravan continued as before and Mum planted the garden with all kinds of vegetables and fruit, so we were never short of fresh produce for the table. She began to keep chickens too, so I soon became used to feeding them and collecting their eggs. Any surplus produce was made into jams, chutneys and preserves and Mum began to experiment with wine-making, using everything from rhubarb to elder flowers. Some were heavenly nectar and others would probably have made battery acid taste good – but anyway, she persevered. We weren't completely self-sufficient but at least everything we ate was super-fresh and full of goodness. The only food we had to buy was bread from the village bakery or Skaith's corner shop and a little meat from the butcher.

When in season, apples and gooseberries were picked by the bucketful and I have memories of an aching stomach after gorging myself in apple-eating competitions. Sister Sue and I would climb up to sit on the rounded top of the old brick wall separating us from the fat pink pigs in Harley's yard. Precariously balanced, with a long drop down into their grubby domain, we would aim apple cores at the grunting monsters. It made us giggle and I'm sure the pigs enjoyed these occasional treats too.

By this time in the1950s we had our first telephone and the number is forever etched in my memory. Telephony was still quite a novelty and formalities were observed. Mum would answer the phone quite nervously, saying very slowly and clearly, 'Hello, this is Waddington 365'. The large Bakelite set was rarely used for idle chatter and we children were not allowed anywhere near it until several years later. Even then we would have to ask permission to use it which would only be granted if the call was important.

As well as phones, more private cars were beginning to appear in and around the village. Ever since his boyhood experiences with Yankee Gilyatt's motor cycle Dad had shown a keen interest in all things mechanical so, if his long legs weren't seen sticking out from under a broken-down truck, they were likely to be writhing underneath a rusty old car. He had learned to drive and maintain all manner of vehicles in the army during the war, before the days of the driving test as we know it, so, although he had a licence, he had never taken a test. He was a highly skilled welder and a perfectionist and, in the little spare time he had, he would bring old cars back to life. I don't remember any of the early ones but he certainly had resurrected an Austin Ruby, which was effectively a tiny Austin Seven and a Singer Le Mans, amongst others, dating from the 1930s.

The next family project, apart from the daily routine of running the business, was to create a larger living space and to dispose of the trusty home-made caravan. The barn was to provide the space so Dad began building an upper floor to create a living area above the workshop with a wooden staircase at the far end. He had been doing some post-war demolition work at R.A.F. Waddington and had cleared out surplus aircraft engine cases made of stout timber. These were huge strong boxes designed to protect the famous Rolls-Royce Merlin engines and the like during transportation and the timber made perfect floorboards for the new accommodation. Steel-framed windows from wartime Nissen huts also provided ideal windows for the new abode.

He built partition walls to create a small W.C at the top of the stairs, a small kitchen, a main living and eating area with a coke stove and a couple of bedrooms. This cosy dwelling was very basic but had all the essentials. It had electric lighting and was a great improvement on the caravan. Although there was no bathroom, we used the kitchen sink for washing and bathed in a galvanised tin bath in front of the stove. I remember 'the flat', as we rather grandly called it, as a very comfortable, happy place and it overlooked the crew yard of the farm next door. If the windows were open, farmyard smells drifted in but I have memories of munching my breakfast whilst watching the cows down below in Harley's farm, contentedly doing the same in their straw-filled yard.

There were very few flushing toilets around in early fifties rural Lincolnshire so the motorised 'dilly cart' was a common site. Whenever it approached, crewed by the 'dilly men' village kids would hold their noses and pull faces as the smelly waste was pumped from all manner of earth closets, tanks and cess pits into the tanker and taken away. My mother insisted that I was washed every day, my teeth were cleaned and hair brushed which of course, like most kids, I hated. As soon as I was outdoors, which was most of the time, I was messing about in dust and dirt, eating ripe fruit straight off the bushes, grazing my knees and exploring the fascinating natural world of spiders, beetles, slugs, snails and all manner of buzzing and crawling things.

Conventional toys were virtually unknown. I had a teddy bear to sleep with in my early years – known simply as Ted – and he was handed on to my sister and eventually, totally threadbare, to my younger brother. I also remember a blue and red toy tanker-truck made of tinplate, which I spent hours pushing to and fro making brrrrum brrrrum noises whilst kneeling in the dirt. Apart from those, I simply amused myself with whatever was at hand; pebbles, sticks, bits of metal, string and so on. Clothes were generally second-hand, passed on to other children or hand-knitted by my mother or my Nan (we always called my paternal grandmother Nan and my maternal grandmother Grandma). Sweaters were un-picked and re-knitted again and again. Little was ever wasted.

In the spring of 1956 Nan came to stay with us in the flat. My mother had mysteriously gone away to hospital in Lincoln and, at five years old, her absence meant little to me. Anyway I always enjoyed being with my Nan. She was funny and used to tell me stories about my dad and how naughty he was when he was little. After a while Mum returned with a little baby, my brother Fred. There had been problems with the birth because he was what is known as a 'blue baby', meaning that he had a condition affecting the oxygen transportation in his blood. It was just as well that she gave birth in hospital because I later learned that this had been a serious life-threatening situation which entailed blood transfusions and intensive care. Fortunately all ended well and the novelty of my new brother being blue was certainly intriguing – although he seemed pink enough to me and no different from the few other babies I'd seen in my short life.

Before my mother went into hospital, we had been given some fertile goose eggs. These were placed on straw in a cardboard box in a warm place near the stove to be sat on by one of our more experienced and trustworthy hens. Tim the cat had to be kept well out of the way during the incubation, but, lo-and-behold, the eggs hatched and, whilst Mum was away producing my brother, other lives had burst into our world and tiny yellow goslings were running around our home.

My brother was christened Robert Frederick after both my grandfathers, Robert – or Bob - Ogden, on my mother's side and Frederick after Fred Dixon Waite on my father's side. Mum called my brother Rob (or Robert if she was angry with him) throughout her life whereas, to everybody else he has always been Fred. She also called my father Ken, when he was otherwise universally known as Les. Whilst on the subject of names, I was sometimes addressed as 'Peebee' and that was occasionally used by my mum even into ripe old age. This name originated because my little sister could not say Peter. I suppose it could have been worse.

The chicken and egg situation was developing and we now had dozens of laying hens, bantams, a few mischievous geese and, a later arrival, a very self-assertive and large cockerel called Brutus. I had a deep respect for (and I must admit, fear of) Brutus. He was a magnificent specimen in his gold and red and emerald plumage with piercing eyes and a large wobbling coxcomb. He had an arrogant strut about him and he certainly 'ruled the roost'. Brutus was not to be tangled with and he seemingly had no fear of humans, or any other living thing, as his raucous crowing would remind us on a daily basis. Fortunately he lived in a wire chicken-run with a selection of his concubines and, unless he had tunnelled out, as he did from time to time, we were able to poke fun at him with impunity.

I have no recollection of what eventually became of Brutus but my parents later had a large wooden hut built and, as a bit of a sideline, kept hundreds of egg-laying chickens in what was known as 'deep litter'. The hens cackled contentedly, running free in the hut and the eggs were collected every day and sold to the Egg Marketing Board to be stamped with the Lion mark ready for retail. Mum and Dad ran this little enterprise for some time but maybe it became unprofitable because the hut, the hens and the arrogant Brutus disappeared a few years later.

Three

Drinking Ink

In September 1955 I started school. After a summer spent in my own little universe, playing in the paddock or shadowing my dad asking endless questions, or watching Mum unpick an old threadbare sweater to re-use the wool, suddenly a whole new world was to open up before me. School. Apart from the first couple of days, I had to walk unaccompanied, sometimes reluctantly, sometimes happily, rain or shine, along the village street to St. Michael's Primary School. I was four and a half years old. From about that age village children were frequently sent alone to the village bakery for a loaf of bread or to post a letter at the Post Office.

It seems irresponsible from today's perspective but we were then still living in an age when everybody in a village was known to everyone else and there was very little traffic. This meant that a small child walking a hundred yards or so to the shop was almost never out of sight of someone who knew them and cared about them. There was even a woman in the village whose only means of transport was a pony and trap. It's hard to imagine how much life has changed.

I had started to read and write a little by the time I began school, thanks to my parents. Despite their busy lives, they always found time to share knowledge with us and, if he wasn't working late, Dad would read us bedtime stories, usually adventures like Treasure Island or Swiss Family Robinson. Grimm's Fairy Tales featuring the likes of Billy Goat Gruff were favourites and Dad would put on suitably scary voices when required.

The school headmaster was Mr Hopkins, known to us as Hoppo. He was larger-than-life, bear-like and a little rotund. We thought he was fat and a bit like Billy Bunter but, probably by today's standards, he was only slightly overweight. Nearly everybody we knew in the 1950s was skinny, so even slightly rounded individuals stood out. He was bald with just a rim of grey-white hair and wore glasses which he was habitually removing and cleaning on a white handkerchief. Despite his bulk, he was expert at sneaking up behind you when least expected – so very little escaped Hoppo's eagle eye.

There were probably about two hundred pupils at the school, divided into four or five classes, so teachers were used to presiding over class sizes of thirty or forty pupils. I remember being in classes of this size well into grammar school. It was fairly usual and the clue to their success is probably in the word 'presiding'. The teachers were most certainly in control. We sat at wooden desks in rows facing the teacher who used a blackboard at the front of the class and we only spoke when asked. When a teacher entered the room, he, or she, said, 'Good morning class' we stood up and droned our reply, 'Good morning Miss', or 'Sir'. A register was taken every day and non-attendance of school for any reason was a serious matter.

For some activities, classes would merge, notably for sport or what was known as 'Music and Movement', when we gathered in the school hall to be put through our paces by a jolly BBC radio voice broadcasted from the little stage. In our raggle-taggle way we waved our arms like the branches of trees, we were little teapots tipping our spouts, we were as small as small can be and as tall as tall can be – and so on. The other radio programme I remember was 'Singing Together' which encouraged us little village urchins to sing traditional folk songs like 'Michael Finnegan', 'Dashing Away with a Smoothing Iron' , 'Men of Harlech' and 'The Lincolnshire Poacher'.

All this was washed down by our daily third-of-a-pint of school milk. These little foil-topped bottles were delivered in crates to all schools in the country to ensure that children had adequate calcium and other nutrients in their diet. The full-cream milk was rich and heavy by today's standards but most kids enjoyed it and soon learned to make rude noises with the paper straws which also doubled as mini pellet-shooters. The bottles were re-cycled again and again so it was usual to see them heavily scratched and worn. In a harsh winter I remember that the milk had frozen solid so the foil tops stood proudly out of the top of the bottle, crowning a column of frozen cream.

Parliament had passed the Free School Milk Act in 1945 under Clement Atlee and every school child under 18 had the right to it until 1968, when the Labour government of Harold Wilson cut it from all secondary schools. The right was then restricted to under-sevens only in 1981 by Margaret Thatcher (then known as Thatcher, the Milk-Snatcher).

The main priorities were the three 'Rs'; reading, writing and arithmetic which we were taught by the 'chalk and talk' method, as it is now somewhat derogatively known. Neatness and spelling were a priority when writing and times tables were chanted aloud ad nauseam. We were given a wood-framed slate at first to write on with a stylus and only when the alphabet was completely mastered were we given thick black pencils and paper. The final stage in learning to write was using a wooden stick pen dipped in black ink which was contained in an ink-well sitting, egg-cup-like, in the top right hand corner of each desk.

This was a big deal and writing with ink in a proper exercise book meant you'd made it.

My dad used to tell me that before I went to school I was a well-behaved little boy but once I started school it was as if a 'silly switch' was pulled and I began to lark about and show off when I went home. Maybe it was a case of letting off steam a little after the discipline in school. I don't especially remember larking around at age four-and-a-half but I do remember a year or so later the first time I was caned..for drinking ink!

Hoppo had left the classroom on some errand. As usual, when the teacher left the room, we were expected to sit quietly until he returned but, this time, I took it into my head to lift the ink-well up to my lips, pretending to drink the ink – causing much hilarity amongst my classmates. Unbeknown to me, when Hoppo had left the classroom, he had padded his way to another one across the yard, from where he still had a good view of my antics. When he returned, we all sat quietly bolt upright as expected but his steely eye homed in on me. I tried denial but it was useless. Firstly, he had seen the entire performance and secondly, the black smudge circling my lips was too much of a giveaway and I was caned. Needless to say, I said nothing to my parents.

Most childhood pranks were pretty harmless – like coating my sister's toothbrush with soap. We learned how to make 'itching powder' from the hairy seeds of rose-hips. A few of them sprinkled down a victim's shirt would result in uncomfortable squirming and a retaliatory punch or two. The wild plant called Cleaver also provided hours of amusement. Also known as 'Stickwilly' or 'Catchweed', the tiny hooks on the seeds and leaves latch onto clothing and hair like grim death. The trick was to attach a large clump of the stuff to the back of someone's jacket or sweater without them realising. This caused much sniggering as the unfortunate victim went about his business with untamed shrubbery apparently growing from his back.

A couple of years into primary school, in 1957, a new boy, Ted Woollan, arrived. He was the youngest son of the new village rector and we quickly became friends. True to his surname, Ted had a woolly mop of untidy blond hair, a kind of rough-and-tumble nature and an adventurous spirit which could sometimes get him, and me, into trouble.

The Rectory was a lovely Georgian house set in mature gardens bordering the school playing field and there were hidden gaps in the fence, allowing small boys to wriggle through. Needless to say, Ted didn't need to walk through the village to school but simply used to appear as if by magic through the secret holes in the fence. On summer evenings and at weekends, the Rectory gardens became our domain. We would make dens out of any old stuff and climb to the top of the mature elms, daring each other to go higher up and further out along branches.

A particular favourite tree was an ageing holly, maybe thirty feet high, which was perfectly cone-shaped with branches reaching down to ground level. By burrowing through these low branches to the inside of the cone which was free of the spiky leaves, we were able then to climb, unseen, right up to the very top of the tree via the main trunk. Once there, we were able to pop out, swaying on the highest flimsy branches, savouring that feeling of excitement, a heady mixture of freedom and fear, knowing that we were in for a great ride down. The 'holly ride' involved simply positioning oneself feet-first on the outside of the prickly branches, committing to the spiky embrace of the tree and just letting go. The friction of the foliage and the angle of the cone shape slowed the rate of fall enough to avoid injury.

If Ted was adventurous, his older brother Geoffrey was, by any stretch of the imagination, madcap in the extreme. He had been packed off to public school but, when at home during holidays, he seemingly spent most of his time getting himself, and his younger sibling, into 'scrapes'. These 'scrapes' were many and varied. I didn't witness all of them by any means, but Ted told me the stories and I did see the resulting effects and scars. These are just a couple of examples. Geoffrey was the proud owner of an air rifle and, having heard stories of William Tell and to demonstrate what a good shot he was, he persuaded Edward to stand in front of a tree with an apple on top of his head. He, Geoffrey, then proceeded to shoot Ted right between his eyes, just above the bridge of his nose. Fortunately, the pellet failed to penetrate his skull. There was blood and a certain loss of pride but it really is a miracle that there was not also the loss of an eye or worse.

One of our favourite boyhood games in the large Georgian rectory was to slide down the polished wooden banisters. This we did at every opportunity when there were no adults around and the interesting part of the ride was the sharp U-bend. Geoffrey decided that this was by no means exciting enough so he declared that he would make the journey down facing FORWARDS. This worked out just fine until he reached the steep U-bend, where he and the banister parted company and he swooped down into the void, smashing into the hall floor where he lay with an injured head and back, but mercifully still alive. The boy was seemingly indestructible and no spell in hospital or punishment deterred him.

The rectory itself was a revelation to me because, at six or seven years old, I had never been inside a large house. Having only lived in a caravan and then the top of a barn, large living rooms, dining rooms, halls, landings and a high-ceilinged kitchen were eye-poppingly impressive and unfamiliar. Ted's father, the Reverend John Woollan, was ex-public school, an ex Royal Navy chaplain and clearly a fairly wealthy and traditional pillar of the Church of England. In the large kitchen, clothes would be placed on a cast-iron, wood-slatted rack and hoisted by pulleys up to the ceiling to dry. Instead of water or orange squash to drink, Ted's mother would give us something called Creamola Foam, different flavours of a magical concoction that really did foam in our mouths. It was wonderful – and they had BROWN bread.

Ted had toys. He had a train set and a game of building bricks with a kind of cement, board games and painting sets. It was a whole new world and what they also had was something called an 'au-pair'. She was a German girl called Monika and Ted told me that, if we looked through the keyhole in her bedroom door, we would be able to see her with no clothes on. I don't know if Ted ever actually managed to see her naked. I assume he *was* speaking from experience and I was certainly intrigued enough to try a few times – but, sadly, without success.

I don't know at what age Ted was sent off to prep school in Dorset but, for small boys, life just goes on in a different way. Of course he was still a playmate during school holidays and then we were as creatively adventurous as before. We tried smoking but, unable to lay our hands on cigarettes, we made our own by rolling dried-up crushed sycamore leaves in newspaper, forming magnificent Churchillian creations. Sometimes these would flare up, seriously threatening hair and eyebrows and at other times they would prove to be damp squibs, sulkily self-extinguishing until we ran out of matches.

The smoking experience was interesting but short-lived. The giant sycamore cigarettes tasted of .. well .. dried leaves and one day, hiding behind a bush, puffing tell-tale clouds of smoke, we were surprised by the Rev Woollan, who confiscated our matches, stamped on our smokes and hoisted us by our collars back into the rectory for a telling-off. He explained to us that smoking inevitably results in something called 'lock-jaw' and he continued to elaborate on this excruciating disease in gory detail and the fact that a painful death would be the eventual and unavoidable outcome. He also explained that, in my case, my parents would not be amused to hear of me smoking, should he choose to tell them, which, the next time he caught me, he would certainly do. I saw the logic of this and, knowing how my dad would take the news and imagining the pain of the punishment, I did not smoke again - and never have, right to the present day.

My pal Ted had left, but life at school continued as before: learning by rote, strict discipline, rushing home for lunch (which we called dinner), cooked by my mother, dawdling back for afternoon classes and back home after school at four o'clock for 'tea' at around five. Playground breaks were very important to us and we played all kinds of games as if our lives depended on them. We played marbles by the high stone churchyard wall, winning, losing, swapping and collecting the beautiful coloured glass balls, which we kept in soft cotton bags, guarding them like the precious sparkling treasures that they were. There was the usual game of 'tag' and another, more active variant which we called 'Sting-'em'. The boy with the ball was the one to avoid. Instead of him chasing as in the game of tag, he pelted an old tennis ball and, once hit – or 'stung', the victim took over the ball – and so on- until playtime ended.

In the autumn term, Conkers reigned supreme. There were mature horse chestnut trees everywhere, all around the village and even hanging conveniently over the school playground from the churchyard, so supply was never a problem. Finding a *prize* conker though was a different matter. It wasn't always about size and shape because sometimes a consistent winner would be fairly small and lumpy – but very hard. There were of course, many theories about 'doctoring' the conker to achieve the necessary toughness and whether soaking in vinegar, slow baking, or other secret treatments did the trick. How to pierce it, string it, the length of string and infinite other variations of preparation were the focus of our obsessions and chatter during the season. It was serious. Our raw and bruised knuckles showed just *how* serious and, as with winning marbles, a 'sixer' or a 'tenner' conker was a treasured possession.

In the playground there was then, and I guess still is nowadays, an informal and unspoken segregation between boys and girls. The girls would be happily skipping and playing hop-scotch, singing and chanting, whilst we boys played our own games, forever teasing, shouting and challenging.

There were one or two slightly tougher games played and the first of these was 'Spread-Eagle'. Many of us, right from an early age and indeed through secondary school, carried knives. This was normal and accepted. Knives were used to whittle and sharpen sticks, make bows and arrows and cut rope and string. They were highly-prized tools, not weapons. We were taught how to sharpen and use them safely by our fathers and I never heard of a single injury through all the eleven or twelve years of primary and secondary school.

Spread-Eagle involved a group of boys standing on grass or soft ground facing each other or in a loose circle, each taking turns to throw the knife so as to stick in the ground away from the feet of an opponent. The opponent would then have to stretch his stance to the knife. I don't remember the details but a). The knife had to stick properly in the earth and b). a player who could not stretch to reach the knife with his toe was out.

A slightly rougher game was British Bulldog which was a real test of speed, agility and courage. It sometimes became too rough and was banned by some schools throughout the sixties and thereafter. If I remember correctly, it involved players lining up against a wall on one side of the playground with one person in the middle of the area. The object was to run from one side to the other without being 'tagged' by the boy in the middle. Anyone tagged then joined the middle player and so on until, as the game progressed from wall to wall, every player was in the middle except one – the winner. It's easy to imagine say twenty boys in the middle and the last two trying to get from one side to the other to become the winner. Tags often developed into thumps and falls. Bruises and grazes were common.

Of course there were organised sports too. Football in the winter and cricket in the summer, as well as the annual end-of-year sports day with all the usual running, jumping, throwing events and sack races. I remember that football boots were a bit of an issue for me. Almost all of our family possessions were second-hand, bought in auction rooms in Lincoln or at jumble sales and my first pair of football boots were no exception. First of all, I don't think they were football boots at all, but were in fact ancient brown leather rugby boots, probably Victorian and laced right up well above the ankle. They were also a size or two too large so they flapped loosely at the ends of my skinny little legs and the hard, rounded toe-ends were turned upwards like circus clowns' shoes. Even at seven or eight years old I felt embarrassed. I know one shouldn't blame the equipment but, wearing my comic boots, I was never going to be a nifty player especially since the games teacher told me that the correct way to connect with the ball was with the top of the boot. This was impossible with such a high boot with turned-up toes.

To cap it all, although the boots flapped loosely, even with an extra pair of socks, over time the nails from the leather studs worked their way through to the inside and I had to put the boots on a makeshift 'last' now and again to flatten them off again with a hammer. All this combined to affect my gait in a particular way. As we all know, football for small boys is simply a chase after a ball with the potential bonus of scoring. The ball is everything and there was the familiar spectacle of twenty or so small boys mobbing the ball like a swarm of bees, blithely oblivious to any idea of passing it or holding a position. It was quite something – especially if the main swarm was being dogged by a slower, awkward-looking, bandy-legged straggler. The ever more urgent whistle-blasts and shouts of the games teacher were a complete waste of time.

As for cricket .. well, if you weren't batting or bowling, it was just a matter of hanging around, making daisy-chains, kicking dandelion clocks and pulling faces at the other bored loafers.

Four

Sticks and Stones

Ted and I were still re-united during holidays when our adventures and explorations resumed. We formed a secret club called 'The Commando Camping Club' (The CCC) with a membership of two, dedicated to honing our outdoor skills of hunting, bushcraft, camping and so on. Ted's father, Rev. Woollan had an acquaintance who lived in Hackthorn Hall, just north of Lincoln and, one summer, we were given permission to camp in the parkland of the private estate. I don't remember much about our stay there under canvas except that we went into the walled garden and bought a bucketful of gooseberries for a few pennies from the head gardener. These we stewed and ate until we could stand no more. How else we survived I don't know but we seemed to take quite easily to sleeping in our little tent in the middle of nowhere, talking and sniggering well into the night.

During our wanderings around the estate, we spotted a large swarm of bees hanging from a branch like a sack of humbugs. It was intriguing for us to see the thousands of buzzing insects in a great pendulous mass covering their invisible queen. We fetched the gardener, who then telephoned a local bee-keeper and we were treated to the spectacle of a white-hooded spaceman puffing white smoke from a canister and scooping up the swarm to be taken off to a new hive. In general, we were left to our own devices for those few days but I imagine, behind the scenes, the gardener or somebody had been asked to keep an eye on us until we were collected at the end of our stay by the Rev in his ageing Humber Hawk saloon.

I was, by this time, a member of Waddington church choir. My parents were not church-goers but, as children, we were assured that church was good for us and we were packed off on each Sunday morning with sixpence for the collection box. I suppose it did no harm and allowed us, in our own good time, to make up our minds about our beliefs. I do remember that the church's sixpence sometimes ended up in the new chewing gum machine outside Read's village shop. Anyhow, although I found the services and sermons boring, I quite enjoyed the singing and the comradeship and the pranks in the choir stalls and I especially enjoyed the weddings and funerals for which we were paid half a crown (12 ½ p) apiece.

Easily the best thing about being in the choir however was the annual church camp in Oxfordshire. In a previous life Rev Woollan had had some connection with Kingham Hill School, a private school which had its own farm and was beautifully situated in the gently rolling Oxfordshire countryside. He had permission to use one of the fields and some facilities for his church camp for a couple of weeks in the summer holidays. We were supervised by a handful of adults namely Rev Woollan, his curate, Stephen, someone called Leo and a couple of the men from the choir. One of these older choir-men was Mr. Philips who was a very kind and patient man. I remember that I, along with another two boys, was taken down to the camp by Mr Philips in his Sunbeam Talbot 90 which had a very luxurious wood and leather interior.

In those days the best route from our part of Lincolnshire to the Cotswolds was straight down the route of the Roman Fosse Way. Once south of Leicester, this route, which is nowadays a very congested trunk road, dwindled into a single-lane gated byway. It was almost dead straight, as most Roman roads are and, now and again, I would have to climb out of the Sunbeam to open and close the farm gates. It was rare to meet another vehicle on this delightful road apart from the occasional farm tractor. The ancient road ran all the way south to the old Roman town of Isca Dumnoniorum, (modern Exeter) but to reach Kingham we didn't have to go that far south.

These camps were great adventures for young boys and were run on loosely military lines. The camp centred on a small marquee which was used for gatherings and meals next to a camp fire with a small supply tent. This was surrounded by four or five ex-army bell-tents where we slept, anything up to ten boys per tent, heads to the outside and toes to the centre pole. The tents were given numbers and working parties corresponded to these numbers. Competition between the tents was encouraged and we had to submit ourselves to kit inspection each day. Assuming the weather was fine, we would have to roll up the walls of the tents (which I seem to remember we called 'braylings') to allow air to flow through. We laid out our kit, neatly folded on our individual groundsheets and we would whittle sticks into shoe-racks, boot-scrapers and the like for which we were awarded points. One of the first jobs on arrival was to dig the latrines over which we built log seats and erected tents.

There were plenty of organised activities and I especially liked the 'night exercises' when we would be in small groups of either 'hunters' or 'prey'. Each group was given a flashlight, a sketch map of the area and a compass. The prey group would be sent out into the woods and fields to hide and, maybe fifteen minutes later, the hunter group would follow in search of them.

There was a boundary marked on the map and a time limit, so really it was just a version of hide-and-seek, but in darkness.

I have memories of sitting round a roaring campfire eating stew and potatoes followed by spooky stories and campfire songs; 'Ten Green Bottles', 'Green Grow the Rushes-O', 'Ging-Gang-Goolie' and all the rest. Sometimes, if it was windy enough, there was a huge white cotton kite with miles of string. Someone would tie a flashlight to it and we would fly it as high as possible, watching the light swing and swoop in the darkness and climb towards the stars.

There was always a den-making contest too and competition was fierce between the teams to make the best-hidden and most elaborate shelter. The school had an outdoor swimming pool which we were allowed to use but there was also an abandoned disused pool surrounded by a high mossy dilapidated brick wall with one old peeling wooden gate in it. It was like entering another world, a magical aquatic wonderland within a walled garden, overgrown with grass and wild plants and the pool itself was half-silted up with sandy mud. Small fish, frogs and newts had found their way into this peaceful lagoon and swimming there was much more exciting than in the new pool. It always felt warmer too, maybe because of the blanket of silt and weeds.

Whilst the annual church camp was a real adventure for me and I loved regaling my parents with tales of my daring deeds whilst away, there was still plenty to interest me at home too. In Lincoln there was a shop called Nobbs. There was also an 'Army Stores' and a scrap merchant known as Sid Twell so, if you needed elastic for your catapult, or maggots for fishing, or a pocket-knife, those were the places to head for. I still have a sheath-knife with a Sheffield blade and a horn handle bought from 'Nobbies' back in the early sixties. Dad made me bows and arrows and catapults and taught me how to carve sticks.

He was his usual creative self when it came to toys and he made us adjustable stilts, so we kids became quite skilful at walking tall. He also invented a thing we knew simply as 'the rocker'. It was a piece of genius welded from steel tubing, with a plank seat, footrests and two handle bars. Painted a deep red, the design meant that it could be ridden by one child or two. It was a thing of beauty and I have never seen one like it anywhere since. He should have marketed it or at least registered the design and made a fortune.

The family business was doing well and there were now, as well as assorted pumps, jack-hammers and compressors, several trucks, each painted in the new company grey and red livery. I recall standing and watching spellbound as a skilled signwriter hand-painted 'Blades and Waite Ltd' with the telephone number on the cab doors and I suppose that this skill has now largely been superceded by transfers and prints. The old cottage at the front of the yard was now empty and in such a bad state of repair that Dad decided to demolish it and build a new house using as many of the materials as possible. At the same time Ray acquired a plot just down the street as the site for a new bungalow. Both of these building projects were completed with the invaluable help of Tom Rowley, the local stonemason and Tommy Brewer, a highly skilled carpenter and joiner. Brian Lockwood, the cowboy who I suspect threw the brick that had 'baptised' me a few years earlier, acted as labourer and, before too long our family had a wonderful new house built in the traditional creamy Lincolnshire limestone.

One small added touch was that my parents made a 'time capsule' using a glass sweetie-jar filled with a few contemporary odds and ends. My memory is unclear but I believe there were family photographs, a few coins, a written message and maybe locks of our hair. This was then built in to the stone wall of the house. I remember exactly where it was entombed and I would be able to go and point to the exact place even now. The house was our first real family home and it was, as far as we were concerned, the height of luxury. It had three bedrooms, a proper bathroom with a flush toilet, a kitchen with built-in units, a garage and a very small stone-walled lawn and garden. My parents must have really thought that they had 'arrived'.

With the expansion of the business in the late 1950s came the first employees and the first character I remember was known to us as Mr Mallet and, over time, he was followed by others. Of course, in those days, drivers did more than just drive. They had to be willing to use a pick and shovel and had to use all kinds of small plant and machinery. We children got to know these men quite well and they in turn grew used to us being around in school holidays, hiding in woodpiles, digging in the dirt and generally getting in the way as they worked, cleaning and repairing their vehicles.

I remember scrounging old nuts, washers and bolts from the workshop to make 'cap-bombs'. By arranging a series of nuts and washers on the bolt, it was possible to insert penny percussion caps, used for toy guns, in between the washers. Having adjusted the tightness, it would be hurled aloft, to land on any hard surface, exploding the caps. The aim was to insert as many caps as possible to create the loudest explosion! With all that heavy metal flying about, it was lucky that nobody was seriously hurt.

I don't know exactly what happened but something must have gone missing from the yard. Thieving was rare but my dad always said that it always seemed to coincide with the arrival of gypsies in the area. An old woman would knock on the door offering to tell your fortune or give you her blessing for a piece of silver and, as if by magic, within a few days, something would disappear. The answer was a guard dog and we soon found ourselves the proud owners of Ben who quickly grew into a magnificent gangly black specimen. He was a jet black Labrador but there must have been a touch of Alsatian or Wolf Hound in him too, because he was tall and lean.

Ben was also the most soft and gentle guard dog the world has ever seen – but he did have a very deep loud bark if there were strangers about at night – so he may well have been effective to some degree. He was an outdoor dog and at night he was chained up and slept in a kennel just inside the yard entrance. Technically he was a working dog, but he also worked his way into our family and, in the worst of winter weather, he would be allowed to come into the house to sleep on the kitchen floor by the Rayburn cooker.

In the winter months we always had a period of snow and ice so, as well as the usual snowball fights, building of snowmen and attempts at building igloos, the kids and families of the village would go sledging down the hillsides facing the Trent Valley. Our sledges were of course always home-built and there was lively debate as to the best design, the fastest sort of metal runners and so on. One particularly hard winter Dad became so enthusiastic that he decided to build a family-sized sledge that would carry both parents and all three children. It was a gem of a design and incorporated, in front of the main runners, a pair of parallel 'steering runners' that were controlled by reins and the driver's feet. It went like the clappers, especially when fully laden, but the steering was hit-and-miss, especially on the black sheet-ice of Milking Hill. The other huge drawback with the family sledge was its sheer weight. Hauling the monster back uphill was a back-breaking task, even with the help of Ben, who was hitched to the reins and seemed to enjoy the challenge. Sadly, Dad admitted defeat and we reverted to our original smaller, lighter individual sledges and he gave the monster to a gang of very keen village youths who couldn't believe their luck.

It didn't last long though because we heard that they had very soon smashed it to pieces by careering out of control into a dry stone wall.

When winter melted into spring, we once again took to the pleasures of hunting for birds' eggs, making dens, collecting tadpoles, fishing for newts, playing with catapults and bows and arrows, making pea-shooters and whistling by blowing across blades of sharp grass. The village was our adventure playground, from the ruin of Brumby's windmill in the south, to the humps and hollows of 'The Ironstone' in the north and all the village lanes in between. Even now I could draw a sketch map of the lanes with their names giving clues to their origins: Tinker's Lane, Capps Lane, Blind Lane, with its sharp ninety-degree bend, Timms Lane, Manor Lane and Far Lane (the sign often defaced by village urchins with a scrawled 'T' to read Fart Lane), Stone Lane, Malt Kiln Lane and Hill Top.

This was my familiar world, the world I had been born into, but it was evolving and growing. Instead of the self-sufficient working village of old, it was becoming a dormitory for the city of Lincoln, only a few miles to the north. A local builder, George Roberts bought up land and began building bungalows, forming small estates which began to surround the old stone heart of the place. The building and expansion continued steadily through the sixties, seventies and eighties right until the present day.

As a family we knew most people in the village but, of course, some were closer than others. Just along the High Street lived Joe and Jean Russell with their young son Richard. Joe and Jean made their living from a mobile fish and chip van which they drove all around the local villages, puffing out clouds of oily steam from the red hot fryer through a tin chimney on its roof. A small fish and chip shop owned by a Polish man called Jachimowicz (I think) had opened in Waddington High Street.

But Joe Russell took the initiative and, by driving his mobile shop with its distinctive delicious smell of cooking chips and vinegar to a wider audience in surrounding villages, he had developed a large and devoted clientele. Richard was one of our playmates and I was always happy to be invited into Mrs Russell's kitchen because she treated me to fizzy pop – sparkling Tizer, orange-flavoured Jusoda and, best of all, Dandelion and Burdock. This was a real treat but drinking it was risky. If you had a fit of the giggles, it would fizz right back up your nose, making your eyes water.

The Barnaby family lived down Timms Lane and my brother and sister became close friends of their children, Peter and Sibyl. Mr Barnaby, who bore some resemblance to Woody Allen, was an art teacher and the house was always a den of creative projects and paintings. He bought an old motor cycle for riding to work in Lincoln and he always gave the impression of being out of control, so other road users gave him a wide berth at all times. I recall seeing him suddenly veer off the Grantham Road one day into the overgrown verge. He fell sideways off the machine, which was revving furiously and spent the next few minutes thrashing about in the tall cow-parsley in a wild attempt to extract the bike. As the fifties became the sixties, there were other motor bikers in the village and they had a habit of meeting on the corner of the lane outside Reid's shop trying their damnedest to look menacing in their black leather jackets and oily jeans. They rode old Triumphs, BSAs and Nortons and their scrawny leader was known as 'Wiggy'. I never knew his real name but he had a greased-back quiff and a pronounced limp, as many bikers seemed to have - and he was, despite his best efforts, absolutely charming.

Five

The Quarry

We must have lived in the stone house at Farrier's Yard for only a few years because, in 1962 our family made another move. It will have roughly coincided with a change of school too, because I found myself at the new St Clements Primary School on Mere Road, which was one of the access routes into Waddington R.A.F. base. The staff also moved so we were still presided over by Hoppo and my favourite teacher, Mr. Caunt, was still trying to inspire us with nature study, geography and history as well as English and maths. He was that rare breed of teachers who, seemingly effortlessly and without any fuss, kept us in line by making any subject interesting. There was humour, intelligence and patience with those who were slow to learn, combined with a perfectly-balanced friendly discipline. The man deserved a medal.

Dad had been removing stone from Mark Howden's quarry on-and-off for several years and he had enjoyed a good relationship with the old recluse. Sadly however, Mark had died suddenly, having lived to a good age in self-imposed solitary confinement in a single room - the kitchen, of his old Victorian family home, Stonefield House. There was no supply of running water, except for what came from a hand-pump which drew rainwater from an underground cistern - and no electricity. In the back garden was a brick outbuilding housing the earth-closet or privy and the whole place was close to being derelict. There were leaking gutters and rotting window frames and vegetation had even grown from the ground floor, right through a front bedroom to emerge at roof level. The grounds had become so overgrown that the place was all but invisible from the road. The house was in such a poor state that Dad, always one for a challenge, *had* to buy it, quarry and all. In fact, the shell of the old house was still very sound, built solidly of dressed stone from the quarry, but it badly needed nursing back to life.

The expanding business had all but outgrown its High Street yard so the quarry provided the perfect solution. The arrangement was that our family would have the old house and garden and Ray's family would have a large plot to build another bungalow. There was plenty of space and there were even a few stone outbuildings, including disused stables that would convert into an office for the business.

A ruined lime-kiln was situated in the shade of a pair of ancient cherry trees so it seems that lime was processed from the quarry at one time, presumably to supply local farms and businesses. The house had to be gutted and there were furnishings and contents, most of which were in such a state of decay that they had to be burnt, including a worm-infested, no doubt once-beautiful, Victorian half-tester bed. As soon as the house was partially habitable, we moved in and the rest of the work progressed with our family in residence.

There were two tragic incidents at around this time that severely affected our family. The first involved one of the truck drivers called Noel Tye, a cheerful former farm worker who spoke with a strong Lincolnshire accent. He was heading back from the coast, having delivered his load and he spotted another Blades & Waite truck coming towards him. It was time for their morning break so they both stopped in a lay-by for a cup of tea and a chat. They were parked nose-to-nose and Noel was between the two trucks, leaning against the bumper, clutching his flask of tea. At this very moment, another vehicle came along that stretch of road and the driver blacked out at the wheel. He had probably suffered a heart attack and he crashed into the back of one of the parked trucks, crushing poor Noel between the two and killing him outright. I don't think that we children were old enough to appreciate the depth of this tragedy but it must have affected my parents and everyone in the company terribly at the time. Noel's wife and family must have been devastated.

The second event concerned Ben, our trusty gentle guard dog and family friend. If he had one fault, it was that he was a very sociable wanderer. Given the slightest chance of meeting a lady-friend, or just a particularly interesting mongrel anywhere in the village, he would be gone. As our close neighbour, Margaret Harrod, said to my mum after one such disappearance, 'Well, Betty .. he's only human!'

However, one day, my sister Sue was taking him for a walk along the Grantham Road on his lead. A farmer drove by in his Land Rover on the other side of the road with a sheepdog in the back. Ben spotted the dog and, quick as a flash, jumped into the road, tearing the lead from Sue's grip. Unfortunately, he ran right in front of another on-coming car and was killed instantly. Sue was very shaken and we were all upset - but none more than my dad. It was the only time I ever saw him cry.

After some time, the gentle Ben was replaced by a new young guard dog, another black Labrador mix, who we named - goodness knows why – Simon. He turned out to be a different character altogether and, whilst he was tolerant of the other members of his pack, i.e. our family, he was a fairly nasty piece of work where visitors were concerned. I suppose, in that sense, Simon had read the job description of 'guard dog' more keenly than Ben had and he threw himself into the role with gusto. He wasn't pretty either. Where Ben had had a gentle face and handled himself with a certain grace, Simon quickly lost half the hair on his pointed snout, giving it the look of polished black leather and he had the calculated economy of movement of a salt-water crocodile. We sort-of liked Simon but that's as far as it went because we couldn't really trust him. It was therefore decided that he needed to be on a chain to act as a deterrent without giving him the freedom to savage anything that moved.

The driveway down to the quarry was about a hundred yards long so it was decided to site his kennel half-way along. From the kennel to the mouth of the quarry a tight wire was rigged up to which Simon's chain was attached, giving him the freedom to patrol the remaining fifty-yard stretch whilst still restrained. One day, a youth on a motorcycle had a delivery for the company and he cautiously revved his way down the first section of the drive. He saw the kennel with the black dog chained close by and he thought, understandably, 'If I put a spurt on, I'll be past the mutt, before he realises'. Sadly for him, he hadn't noticed the running–wire so, just as he put the 'spurt' on, Simon spotted his victim..and charged. Bounding up onto the back of the bike, the beast sank his teeth into the back of the rider's leather jacket.

The interesting spectacle of a motorcycle with a rider and a snarling dog riding pillion only lasted for a few seconds because, at the end of the wire run, the motorcycle sped happily onwards. Simon's chain snapped tight with dog attached, still clenching a large shred of leather jacket in his teeth and the hapless young rider was dragged from his machine into the dust. Fortunately, apart from being badly shaken up, the lad and his motorbike were un-damaged. He was dusted down, given a cup of tea and compensated to the tune of a new jacket, so all was well. Simon's pride was hurt and I suspect he never really came to terms with the injustice of being half strangled for simply doing his job.

The move in to Stonefield House meant that we were closer to the R.A.F. station which was now playing an important role in the United Kingdom's nuclear deterrent. We had become used to the sight and the ground-shaking noise of the awesome four-engined Vulcan bombers being put through their paces day and night. In the early years they were painted pure white for high-level attack but, from the mid 1960s onwards, their imposing delta-shaped bodies were re-painted in camouflage colours. The Soviet Union's improved SAM missiles meant that the 'V' bombers could no longer rely on speed and height for protection, so low-level, under-the-radar tactics were introduced. The crews were trained to fly at little more than tree-top height at the speed of sound and I have vivid memories of almost jumping out of my skin when one of these monsters suddenly blasted the sky apart right above my head.

From the 16th to the 28th October 1962, when I was eleven years old, the world faced the real and grave threat of total nuclear war as Nikita Khrushchev and John Kennedy played their dangerous game of chicken. The Cuban Missile Crisis meant that, for a few nights, the Vulcans of Waddington were especially active. They were loaded with nuclear weapons and ready, around the clock, to go to attack Russia, with the chilling likelihood of never returning home. Our parents tried to explain that something important was happening whilst, at the same time, reassuring us that we were quite safe as we lay awake in our beds listening to the constant thunder of those Olympus jet engines. Fortunately, after the stand-off, common sense prevailed and the Vulcans resumed their usual, noisy but harmless, mock attacks over the wide skies of the east of England.

The quarry was becoming increasingly busy. Business was booming and the expanding plant-hire activities meant that a new workshop had been built and there were all kinds of machines around the place. There were tracked Drott diggers, JCBs, 360-degree Atlas diggers, low-loader trucks to transport them, bull-dozers, compressors, pumps, generators, jack-hammers, tipper-trucks and service vans. Dad and Ray were bidding for and carrying out demolition work, especially associated with the post-war dismantling and alteration of the many R.A.F. bases in the area.

One such base was R.A.F. Faldingworth to the north-east of Lincoln which had been active during the war but was then adapted to become a weapons storage facility, holding nuclear weapons for the surrounding bomber bases. The demolition work meant that any useful reclaimed materials were brought back to the quarry for storage ready to use or sell on. These materials included many hundreds of sheets of asbestos which were cut, broken and handled with no knowledge of the hazardous nature of the substance. Another lucrative line of work was 'dyking'. A dyke, or dike, generally means a wall or embankment built to prevent flooding but, in Lincolnshire, it is the exact opposite - a ditch. Maintaining and expanding the network of dikes, especially in the low-lying fens, was an important job and it provided a great deal of work for Blades & Waite.

All this meant more employment and the workforce increased steadily throughout the sixties and seventies up to twenty or thirty men and a secretary called Sheila who worked with my Grandad in the office. Some of these characters stick in my memory: Horace Brumby, who chain-smoked Woodbines, kept pigs and owned the ruined windmill at the end of the village, Jim O'Hare with his soft Irish brogue, John Goy, a man of few words who was the highly-skilled driver of an old-fashioned 10RB excavator used for deep-diking, sometimes adapted for demolition by attaching a wrecking-ball, Tom Brummitt the truck driver, the two Lens (Scott and Kirk) who were Drott drivers and Gordon Allen, the black-bearded piratical workshop manager.

Most of the drivers had begun their working lives on Lincolnshire farms so they were not afraid of hard work in all weather conditions and some spoke with the strong dialect of the county. A really strong Lincolnshire dialect is seldom heard nowadays but when I was young it was not uncommon to hear locals deep in a conversation which was all but indecipherable to an outsider. I will attempt a phonetic version of a typical exchange between a couple of farmers meeting on market day.

'Neear then meate, I 'ent seen yer ovver a munth er more, e-yer arl rate?'

'Yis surrey, I bin liftin' teates deown bottom but, wot wi'the kelchin' we've 'ed, it's bin a rate struggle.'

'Aye, that theer nearber o' yourn sez it's bin silin' deown, an' wi' that claggy-owd greound they're near rott'n afore yer start. Tracters wearn't git thruffer the geate n' likely iz yer'll end up stuck fast, like, in th'edge-bottom.'

Roughly translated, they were saying, 'Hello mate, I haven't seen you for at least a month. Are you OK?'

'Yes, I've been harvesting potatoes down in the valley but the wet weather has made it difficult.'

'Yes, your neighbour told me it's been pouring and, in that heavy clay soil, the crop is almost rotten before you start. Tractors are unable to get through the gate onto the land and you're likely to end up getting stuck in a ditch.'

In some cases, for instance that of Herbert Cragg, the village 'odd-job' man and scruffy eccentric, speech was rendered virtually pointless by the strong dialect being coupled with the tatty dog-end of a cigarette which was a permanent fixture on his bottom lip, muffling and slurring any attempt at conversation.

This, coupled with the coughing and spitting, caused by his chain-smoking.

Family life continued much as before except that we now enjoyed more living space. The overgrown grounds had been tamed and we now had lawns, surrounded by mature elms, beeches and a rare weeping-ash tree. My mother created a well-tended vegetable patch with a greenhouse and we children were encouraged to grow little rows of radishes and carrots. A time came when Dad developed an interest in playing tennis. He had a friend in the village called Vernon Chapple, who lived in a large house overlooking the Trent Valley. In his garden was a tennis court and he allowed Dad and a few other friends to play there.

I remember going with him sometimes and slowly learning how to play. I was hooked. I had a second-hand varnished wooden Slazenger 'Demon' racket, with a red devil's face on it, strung with 'cat-gut' - and we had to store these wooden rackets in tight presses to prevent them from warping. The love of the game has stayed with me until this day. Those early tennis matches later inspired my father to build a hard court by the vegetable plot in our garden. We developed a family tradition of playing on Christmas Day every year, whatever the weather. It was not unknown for us to scrape snow off the court to allow us to bash a ball about to work up a healthy appetite for a heavy Christmas dinner.

Six

Wheels

Every Saturday late afternoon before dusk in the month of February, Dad would take me (and later, my brother Fred too) off to shoot pigeons in the woods down the hill from Harmston, a neighbouring village. The woods were owned by local farmer, Derek Meanwell and it was the tradition that, throughout Lincolnshire, shooters would cover as much of the county's woodland as possible to kill the birds as they attempted to roost for the night. Keeping them on the move increased the chance of them coming into range of the guns as they tried to enter each wood or copse. Pigeons were, and still are, the curse of arable farmers. They breed like mad and a flock of pigeons feasting on, for instance, a field of young rape-seed plants will completely decimate the crop in a few hours, costing thousands of pounds. Scare-crows and other more humane measures have always proved ineffective and poisoning is certainly not an option.

We would build a hide in the woods from dead branches and sit in complete silence awaiting the arrival of small groups of birds hoping to settle in for the night. I loved these times with Dad, staying so quiet and still that rabbits and songbirds would come very close to us, unwittingly sharing the peace of the woodland. In the distance, faint sporadic pops of shotguns broke the cold silence as flocks descended on other shooters lying in wait just as we were. Then we would hear a rattle of wings and a purr as a few birds settled nearby. Dad would slowly raise his gun and fire. If the target bird was at the limit of his range, he would first use the left-hand choke barrel, giving maximum range and a narrower spread of shot. If that failed, shot from the right hand barrel quickly followed and hopefully, one way or another, the bird was killed, falling to the soft damp ground with a light thump. I acted as a retriever. Pigeon pie, filled out with hard boiled eggs and bacon in a crumbly short-crust pastry case, was a real winter treat for the whole family.

We were taught about guns and knives from an early age. Safety was paramount and you would never point a weapon of any kind at a living thing you did not intend to kill, so a shotgun was only ever loaded when it was likely to be used. Whenever walking, climbing fences and crossing ditches or other obstacles, the gun was 'broken' and unloaded. At all times the muzzle would be pointing at the ground or the sky. When you did actually raise the gun towards a target, you had to be sure that there would be no unseen or unexpected victim behind it. Shooting pigeons in woodland is pretty straightforward because you are always firing from ground level upwards into the trees, with only sky beyond, but in other situations - say shooting a running hare, it is all too easy to focus only on the hare and fail to notice the dog – or worse – the dog-walker, in the shadow of the hedge behind.

Our fathers taught us these things and, when the time came to handle a gun, we did so with the utmost care. I fired my first shot when I was about eleven years old. My father's gun was a trusty old 12-bore with a traditional 'hammer' mechanism. He told me that I had to hold it very tightly against my shoulder but evidently I didn't follow instructions because, when I pulled the trigger, the gun leapt backwards under my armpit and the hammer dug into the bridge of my nose. When we arrived home my mother let out a shriek as she saw me with a mess of congealed blood between my eyes and over my jacket. 'What on earth have you done', she yelled.

'Dad shot me', I said with a grin.

Apart from learning from our parents how to stay safe, we were also instilled with what is now known as 'the work ethic'. We were given pocket money – I seem to remember that it was initially sixpence (i.e. 2½ pence) every Saturday – but only in return for doing jobs. The jobs ranged from dish-washing to chopping kindling for the fire or digging the vegetable plot. Any back-chat or misbehaviour might also mean foregoing the payment on top of any other punishment, depending on the 'crime'. This meant that we three children, in common with most others whom we knew, never expected to receive anything for free and learned that, if you treat people badly or do something dishonest, there will most likely be a price to pay. I know that these simple lessons have stayed with all three of us right to the present day. Not that we didn't push the boundaries as all kids do and I know I was a real handful sometimes for my parents as I became a fully revved-up teenager. Every generation has its own view on what constitutes good behaviour and achieving a balance between consideration for others and self-fulfilment. Certainly, for my generation there was a healthy element of fear - which was, I believe, fundamental in keeping us in line.

In the sixties, Waddington had a village policeman who lived with his family in a small police house on Stone Lane. I have no idea how busy he was but, as far as I was concerned, his mere presence was a real deterrent and the last thing any child wanted was the village bobby turning up on the family doorstep. Similarly, with teachers, that hint of fear meant that they could easily manage large class sizes. The greatest childhood fear was of one's parents getting wind of anything bad because that might well mean no pocket money and being, in today's parlance, 'grounded'. As a last resort and after a single verbal warning, it would mean the back of a hand or the end of a belt. In general, Mum was the comforter and bather of grazed knees and Dad was the judge, jury and punisher. If we were 'trying it on' with Mum, she only had to say 'Just wait until your father gets home..' and that would be enough.

I believe that most of the blame for behavioural problems in children ultimately lies with parents. I could write a full thesis on the subject and probably get myself into a whole lot of trouble expressing 'old-fashioned' views. However, it may well be that, in our current highly-materialistic world where there seems to be an increasing reluctance to consider others or accept personal responsibility, there is still something to learn from the past. The sight of children charging around in a restaurant, yelling and banging plastic toys on tables, 'expressing themselves' whilst their proud parents smile fondly, oblivious to the feelings of any other diners, is all too familiar. It's too easy to blame the government, the council, the teachers or the weather for anything and everything but, as I end this little rant, I remember my Grandfather (my Dad's Dad) telling me once, 'If you can't find anything good to say about someone, boy.. keep your mouth shut'. It was an easy thing for him to say but I really never did hear that man say a bad word about anybody. Now and again I find myself biting my lip, closing my eyes and remembering his advice.

My grandfather's name was Fred Dixon Waite. I know little of his early life but I have an old photograph of him proudly wearing the uniform of the Royal Lincolnshire Regiment. I imagine it was taken just before he went off to fight in the trenches of the First World War. During and after the Second World War, he worked for the Air Ministry, spending some time at a mysterious place called Rudloe Manor and he would set off with a tiny brown suitcase, only returning to his wife at weekends. At some point, when he was a young man, he worked as a footman for the Cunard family (the shipping dynasty). I understand that he was well-liked and well-treated by them and I still have a watercolour depicting hunting dogs, given to him by one of the daughters, signed C.M. Cunard. I never saw him in a bad mood. As a young man, he was a good all-round sportsman, playing football and cricket in local teams. He was fit and strong but, at the same time, gentle and polite with a ready smile. My Nan was a completely different character but they complimented each other perfectly. Where Grandad Fred was a gentle soul, my Nan, Doris, was a feisty and fussy woman, always on-the-go, making him lift his feet to clean under his chair and so on. She loved to gossip and, whilst she stood no nonsense, she had a heart of gold.

For a few years, they moved away from the village to live in a rented house in Cuckney, Nottinghamshire. I sometimes stayed with them during summer holidays and two episodes stick in my mind. The first illustrated her creative genius when it came to dealing with misbehaviour. I have no idea what I had done, maybe stayed out playing too late, or something. She reached into a drawer and pulled out a Nazi Swastika flag. It was a captured flag that my father had brought back from the war. She told me that it was a signal flag and that she only had to hang it out of the upstairs window. The coal-man passing in his lorry would see it and he would know to call in to take me away. It was instantly effective because I, like most kids, eyed the sooty-faced, sweating coal-man with suspicion and fear.

The second incident occurred one very hot day, I had no shirt on and I leaned on a bee that was crawling up the coal-shed door. The sting was excruciating and I remember yelling and Nan dabbing some soothing lotion on my back and telling me not to be a baby. She told me that the bee had had the worst of the deal because it would be destined to crawl off to die. 'Serves it right', I thought. She ran a personal vendetta against all members of the insect world and was the proud owner of a dreaded 'Flit Gun'. No sooner would a stray bluebottle enter her domain than she would declare, 'Right – I'll have to get the Flit!' Out would come what appeared to be a rusty old bicycle pump with an attached battered cylinder containing, no doubt, some substance highly toxic to all living things, including human beings. Muttering something about 'Pesky Critters' under her breath, she would pump for all she was worth, filling the room with a poisonous fog - only happy to stop when the unfortunate fly was lying belly-up.

My first bicycle was a blue Phillips 3-speed sports bike with straight handlebars – second-hand of course. I suppose my friends must have been given their bikes at around the same time and it seemed that now the whole world was open to us. Initially, I just cycled to my friends' houses and here and there around the village. My best friend at the time was Terry Wells whose father was the local painter and decorator and whose mother came from India. Terry took after his mother and he was the only mixed-race person in our school or indeed anywhere in the area. He was a great collector of cigarette cards and postage stamps so I started to collect too and I loved going to his house to compare and swap cards. I also loved going because of the delicious food smells when his mum was cooking. They ate amazing things called curries and I was intrigued. I don't remember ever being offered any to try though, so I assume they just thought I wouldn't like it.

Gradually, the cycling distances grew so that I was soon venturing to all the surrounding villages. We never carried water, even on the hottest summer days, because, in almost every village there was at least one silver-grey pump cast as a column featuring a lion's head with a water-spout sticking out from its mouth. You simply turned the chunky tap on the side for a limitless supply of fresh drinking water. I suppose these were the descendants of the old parish pumps. In Waddington, there were at least two of them and, whilst nowadays we are all buying drinking-water in plastic bottles, then we simply cupped our hands and drank whenever we saw a silver lion.

We learned very quickly how to add an 'engine' to our bikes by clipping a piece of stiff cardboard to the frame using clothes pegs. The card engaged with the wire spokes as they turned, producing a very satisfying brrrrrr.. Oh, the wonders of technology! Of course that drove even us kids mad on a long ride, so the 'engine' was reserved for quick flips around the village. The speed and range of the bikes could be fully exploited to expand our forays into the countryside to search for birds' eggs and also to go down to the river on fishing expeditions. I had a collection of birds' eggs ranging from a little brown-flecked wren's egg to those of pheasants and moorhens. Dad had taught me how to pierce and blow them to remove the yolks. Although I only ever took a single egg from any given nest, this is now illegal - and quite rightly so.

Near the village of Aubourn, south west down the hill from Waddington there used to be a water mill. I arrived too late in the world to ever see it working but, in my time, it was a flattened ruin with just a few of the workings and millstones left as witness to its purpose. What also remained though, was the mill race and the pool that reminded me of John Constable's 'Hay Wain' painting. A beach of sorts had formed from sandy silt and it was an idyllic and peaceful place, perfect for a Sunday picnic. I have very happy memories of one particular family outing where we were joined by Ron Gambles, the farmer and his family. It was a perfect summer day and the water was warm enough for swimming and splashing about in. If you were to walk there now, you would see no sign that there had ever been a water-mill. The pretty mill-pool and race have been replaced by an ugly concrete and steel sluice.

Most boys were interested in fishing and I was no exception. Dad had taught me about the various species of fish and how to go about catching them and I had a friend at school called Robert Kirk who was very keen. Robert's father was a chief technician in the R.A.F. and a key member of a Vulcan bomber crew and the family lived in one of the new village bungalows. Most R.A.F. personnel lived in quarters on the camp and we saw little of them, but a few families opted for village life instead. Sometimes Robert and I would tie fishing rods to the crossbars of our bikes and ride off down to the river which teemed with gudgeon, perch, roach, bream and chub. The fish we really wanted though, was the arch-predator, the pike – and there were some really big ones to be had. We honed our technique and it was not unknown for us to catch large fish weighing from ten to fifteen pounds. I remember once riding home with a pike dangling from each end of my handlebar. We used to prepare them and soak them in salt water before cooking to get rid of any muddiness in the taste and, though a little bony, the flesh was white and sweet.

A year or two before, Dad, with me as his apprentice, had built a two-seater kayak, a fifteen-foot PBK, from plans. I loved learning about the materials, the brass screws and copper nails, how to steam and bend timber, stretch the covering, treat it with dope and varnish and paint. I learned new nautical terms, from prow to stern, keel and keelson to ribs and rubbing strakes. The whole thing was painstakingly assembled and glued to form a floating work of art from canvas and wood. Usually the kayak was strapped on to a roof-rack on the car for family outings to the seaside or to the river, but I knocked up a simple trailer using a pair of old pram wheels and a long metal tube which connected to the seat-stock of my bike. This meant that I was able to tow the boat down to the river independently.

When we weren't fishing, Robert Kirk and I would paddle up and downstream looking for moorhens' nests or trying to spot the lurking pike. We knew of a particular apple tree growing in the middle of a riverside field near Aubourn which, in season, was laden with sweet, bright red fruit. We loaded bag after bag of them into the covered bow and stern of the kayak and paddled on our way. The boat was so overloaded that the water lapped over the deck, against the coaming; the frame of the cockpit. Goodness knows how we managed not to capsize, but I remember slogging homeward up the hill, pushing a bike and a kayak heavy with apples.

As well as learning the new skills of catching fish and boatbuilding, it was not long before I drove a car for the first time. Dad managed to buy a cheap (I suppose it may have set him back around ten or fifteen pounds) 1936 Morris Eight saloon for us children to drive around the dusty yard. The quarry was surrounded by other land reclaimed from rubbish tips so we had a total of about six acres - plenty of space for practising stops, starts and 3-point turns. Of course, this also entailed learning about maintenance and how the engine and other components worked. We were forever fiddling with fuel pumps, spark plugs and dynamos to keep the old thing running. We also had to save up our pocket-money to toddle off down to the local garage with a can to buy petrol at something like 3s 6d a gallon (17½p). When my brother Fred was maybe eleven or twelve, he bought a rusting old Renault Dauphine and then, later on, a BSA motor cycle for charging around on. Of course, we couldn't wait for the day when we would be allowed to drive on the open roads.

Throughout all of these 'extra-curricular' activities, our poor mother had to fight a constant battle to try to keep us clean and tidy. Fred and I were marched off every so often to a barber called Reg Batty a few miles away in Bracebridge Heath, who seemed to relish the prospect of inflicting the mandatory 'short-back-and-sides' on us. On one particular visit, he seemed to be grappling somewhat with Fred's blond mop and at last he produced an unsavoury-looking, hair-covered red globule. 'Do you still want this?', said Reg. Fred looked puzzled but, on closer inspection, it turned out to be the hairy remains of a strawberry-flavoured boiled sweet.

There was also a parental determination that we should look after our teeth so, as well as being instructed in the fine art of teeth-brushing, we were taken off to Mr Gaffney the dentist every six months. He, in common with other N.H.S. dentists of the time, was paid by the number of treatments he performed and so it was pretty well expected that an inspection would consist of the usual poking, scraping and prodding, accompanied by Mr. Gaffney sucking in his breath with relish and tut-tutting as the pound-signs filled his eyes and he added up his potential earnings. When it came to the actual drilling and filling or, even worse, whipping out a few of the little blighters, he didn't mess around with injections or any kind of local anaesthetic. It was straight in with the laughing gas so his victims – sorry - patients – were out for the count and he was free to do what the hell he liked. Thank goodness that nowadays things have changed. The difficulty now is actually *finding* an N.H.S. dentist willing to take you on.

A crucial part of childhood is the testing of limits, as any parent knows only too well. One memorable experiment for my friends and I almost ended in disaster though. It was 1963 and John F. Kennedy had been shot dead on the 22nd of November. It is often said that everyone knows where they were and what they were doing on that day, but we were too young and absorbed with our own childish dramas to be affected by faraway events, no matter how earth-shattering. However, the winter of 1963 went on to become one of the coldest on record in the U.K. The big freeze lasted for weeks up until March and even the sea froze in places. This, of course, meant adventure for village boys and girls who made snowmen and attempted igloos, had snowball fights and ventured onto rivers and ponds to slither and slide.

I and a small gang of friends, including my sister Sue, went down Milking Hill and into a field with a large pond in it. It must have been towards the end of the really cold spell because the ice was covered by a film of water and, although still a few inches thick, cracks were showing. We all merrily jumped onto the slippery surface and began sliding and bouncing around when – snap! – the inevitable happened and a few of us found ourselves in the cold black water, clinging for all we were worth to a steeply-sloping sheet of heavy ice. How we managed to drag ourselves out I have no idea, but it shook us all to the core and I know we all realised what a narrow escape it had been. If we had lost our grip and the ice had closed over our heads, there would most likely have been a few grieving families that night.

Needless to say, there was no hiding that particular episode from our parents because we were soaked from head to foot and were numb and shaking when we eventually reached our homes. I don't remember being punished or lectured for our stupidity so maybe our parents realised that a harsh lesson had been learned, never to be forgotten. In general, the extreme winter weather was a delight for us children but, in the day-to-day lives of working people, especially in the countryside, it meant nothing but hardship. My father's business, along with all other businesses and farms, virtually ground to a halt. Attempts were made to keep the main roads open however and the county council enlisted the help of businesses like ours and farmers to clear snow, so diggers and tractors with snow-ploughs were sent out, often working throughout the night, to cut through drifts three or four metres deep. At least it provided some desperately-needed income.

Seven

Small Fish – Big Pond

In common with all other children of my age, I sat the Eleven-Plus exam in 1962. I had enjoyed most of my schooling, mainly thanks to the valiant efforts of Mr. Caunt and I managed to pass. This meant that, in the September of that year, I began the next stage of my education at North Kesteven Grammar School, a modern state school in North Hykeham, about five miles west of Waddington. Failing the exam would have meant instead starting the new term at the Sir Robert Pattinson Secondary School, also in North Hykeham. Despite all the controversy that surrounded the eleven-plus exam in subsequent years and all the debate about streaming in schools based on ability, I have no recollection of any discord at the time. In fact, the eleven-plus hardly seemed any different from the annual end-of-year tests we sat to check our progress. It was just accepted that 'grammar school kids' would be fed on a diet of literature and Latin, whereas the secondary modern curriculum had a more practical vocational emphasis.

Whatever the school though, the move up into secondary education was, and still is, a big deal for a child. I was used to being close to the top of the food chain in my village primary school but now, suddenly, I found myself mingling with boys who were wearing long trousers and who seemed to know an awful lot more than I did about almost everything. Prior to starting the new school, I had to be rigged out in the new uniform and provided with the correct sports kit and so on. This meant a visit to Wingads School Outfitters in Lincoln with my mother who worked through the list and fussed around while I tried on blazers and rugby shirts. Whereas in primary school, competition was limited to some little swat being dubbed 'top of the class' each year, in our grammar school it was actively encouraged at all levels in conjunction with 'teamwork'.

Suddenly, the idea of twenty scruffy urchins swarming after a football was not acceptable. You had to pass it to your teammates to stand any chance of winning the game. Not only that, there was streaming by ability into Alpha, Beta, Gamma and Delta in each year, as well as division into three 'houses'; Newton, Tennyson and Wesley, mainly used for sporting competitions and named after three famous Lincolnshire-born heroes. I was put in class 1A and the house named after Sir Isaac Newton who, as all schoolboys know, was the man who invented gravity. Without him, we would all be in a real pickle, floating aimlessly around the universe.

Village children were delivered to both of the secondary schools by a shared bus, so I had to join a small group of bleary-eyed companions at the end of Stone Lane each morning waiting to be collected by a jaunty old Bedford sporting the cream and red livery of Hodson's Coaches. If I was kept behind at school for any reason, such as punishment, or if I was just too slow, I would find myself walking the five miles home, which was a slog because Waddington is on top of a limestone ridge and Station Hill is fairly steep. Similarly, when I played rugby or other sport after school, I had to ride there on my trusty blue Phillips bike and home again afterwards. I don't remember ever being delivered or collected by car.

My mum never passed a driving test and my dad was busy working so a 'school run' was out of the question. Incidentally, throughout my schooldays, I have no recollection of our school being closed for any reason during term time. There were no training days or 'Baker' days for teachers, no closures because of bad weather (and we certainly had plenty of that) or for any other reason. The school day began at 9:00 a.m. and ended at 4:00p.m., with a lunch break from 12:20p.m. to 1:50p.m.

'Youth is wasted on the young.' So said either Oscar Wilde or George Bernard Shaw, (depending on whom you believe) and that is certainly true. I didn't appreciate how lucky I was to be given a terrific free education. I knew nothing of starvation or neglect and I took for granted the love and care of my parents and the safety of my surroundings. Fortunately, I was fit and healthy and I, along with my friends, seemed to have limitless energy, spending virtually all of my spare time out in the fresh air. I do remember catching pneumonia though, when I was about fourteen and having to spend a few weeks at home in bed being visited by Doctor Adams. The only up-side was that my mum taught me to knit but, at that age, confinement was very frustrating.

The main business of the school, i.e. stuffing our young heads with as much knowledge as possible, continued relentlessly and I was introduced to the dubious delights of Latin, which was a compulsory subject for the first two years. The teacher was a tall, lanky man called Frank Mason who was a slightly untidy academic, garbed in a chalky threadbare sports jacket a size or two too small for him. Although Mr. Mason was generally an affable sort with a keen sense of humour, his pupils treated him with great respect and a little fear. His imagination ran wild when it came to punishment and his methods certainly wouldn't be tolerated in today's world. It was not unknown for him to rub an eraser up the back of a boy's neck when he failed to remember the conjugation of a certain verb. It always seemed to be boys who were punished. Maybe he was afraid to pick on girls or maybe they always learned their verbs and were well-behaved, I'm not sure.

If you failed to do your homework and couldn't reel off a certain verb, he had a habit of calling you a 'Nit-Wit'. You might be told to write out fifty times, 'I am a Nit-Wit' or, worse, he would pull your hair, forcing you to stand on your chair – or even the desk – and then you would have to shout out the same phrase a dozen or so times to the whole class. 'I am a Nit-Wit. I am a Nit-Wit. I am a Nit-Wit…'. Of course, this would now break every school rule and a few laws too. I assume that, nowadays, any teacher getting anywhere near this kind of behaviour would be instantly fired and probably locked up but, to us, it was fairly normal, if slightly eccentric, discipline.

Latin lessons were usually taken in one of a pair of temporary, Portakabin type, classrooms and the 'standing on the desk' punishment routine came to a sudden end one day however when an accident happened. The story we heard was that Frank was in full flow teaching and a boy had been duly hoisted to the desk top. The pupil began his shameful 'Nit-Wit' chant and then, for some reason, he lost his balance and fell out of the window. Fortunately, he was unhurt but it might well have been a different story if it had not been a ground floor room. The incident didn't signal the end of Frank's inventiveness or firmness and, on another occasion, whilst teaching us, he was shouting and thumping the blackboard so hard that the board in the neighbouring classroom fell off the wall on top of poor Miss Gordon who was semi-concussed whilst trying to teach maths.

There were other tough teachers too who would not hesitate in meteing out physical punishment. Believe it or not, we had a metalwork teacher called Mr. Steel and a woodwork teacher, Mr.

Wood. Mr. Wood was a delight, but I remember Mr. Steel as a bully who wouldn't hesitate in throwing heavy objects or giving a good slap. As at primary school, class sizes were typically thirty to forty and teachers were able to manage them with ease, thanks to the strict discipline and the unwavering support of parents.

Some of the older teachers kept order by simple force of personality. I'm thinking, in particular, of the crow-like Dr. Coles our English master, who was old-school and used to glide into the classroom wearing a long black university gown. The formality of standing when a teacher entered was still observed and he would look down his nose like a high court judge, scanning the room for any sign of insubordination, before telling us to sit. Of course, there were always pranks, even aimed at the most formidable teachers and I remember a few drawing pins being placed on Dr. Coles' chair and stifled sniggers when he settled down on them with no apparent discomfort.

One of the geography teachers was Mr. Pickering, a Yorkshireman who was painfully thin and had a long nose supporting horn-rimmed glasses. He walked with a peculiar backward-leaning gait as if to compensate for the forward mass of the nose. Coupled with his bird-like movements, this gave the overall impression of a strutting chicken and he was simply known as 'The Beak'. He was a pretty good geography teacher but, maybe because of his demeanour, he had no natural authority. However, such teachers were not powerless because they always had the full backing of the school headmaster, Mr. Winwood who was armed with the dreaded cane. One way or another we were kept in line.

We were once on a geography field trip, a day out in the Derbyshire Peak District, learning about rock formations, landscapes and so on. The Beak was stalking ahead of his motley group when he found himself confronted by an electric cattle fence. We all gathered round and he pointed out the hazard and decided to test whether the power was connected by touching the wire with a straw. He held out his bony hand and Ping!.. I've never seen anyone jump like it. I don't remember much about the formation of the landscape but I've always had a healthy respect for electric fences ever since.

The main purpose of a state grammar school was to prepare its pupils for further education at university and, in the process, for a successful career and adult life. The academic pathway centred around 'O'-Levels in several subjects, including compulsory Mathematics and English, and then, if you chose to continue into the sixth-form, 'A'-Levels up to age eighteen. I took eight 'O'-Levels in Mathematics, English Literature, English Language, French, Physics, Chemistry, Biology and Geography. I then took three 'A'-Levels in French, English Literature and Geography. This was fairly typical and an education based on these exams, despite its' many critics, really did provide a sound platform.

Apart from the academic toil, there was encouragement to excel at sport. Girls were expected to play netball and hockey and boys played rugby and cricket. I played rugby in the winter months and played for the house and also sometimes for the school. I was tall and skinny and I certainly didn't have enough killer instinct to play well. There were a few injuries and I remember coming out of a scrum with blood over my face and a neat hole punched through my cheek. In contrast, a Scottish boy from my year called Donald Bathie, was a proper hard-case. Built like a bull, he seemed completely impervious to pain and used to cut through any opposition like a knife through butter.

We were taught how to tackle oncoming players nice and low and tight, but, at the sight of Bathie bearing down on you full-steam-ahead, all theory went out of the window and he would brush you aside as if he were swatting a fly. When I was about fifteen, I was playing quite often on Saturdays for the school but, during one particularly bruising game, I found myself waking up on the touch-line after being knocked out. I realised that I wasn't enjoying it and that I would rather be spending my Saturdays working for my dad and earning a few pounds.

Rugby was for winter and, in summer, cricket replaced it as the main boy's sport. However, both boys and girls had the option of all kinds of athletics events and, being a 'jack-of-all-trades', I was okay at track events and javelin and long-jump, but there were plenty of kids who were better. I did find a little niche for myself though at pole-vault and, in 'Yan-Tan-Tethera', the school magazine of 1967, it says, 'Pole-Vault P. Waite (Newton) 9'3" (record)'. I was a gangly sixteen year old who couldn't handle the tedium of school cricket and being a pole-vaulter meant being left to my own devices to practise, which suited me fine.

The school headmaster, Mr. Winwood, was quite forward-thinking and he was quick in adopting the concept of a sixth form college. This was meant to act as a gentle introduction to further education and so, amongst other things, the rules governing school uniforms were relaxed. We also had a sixth form common room and lessons were more like university lectures. We had been pushing our luck with the school uniform anyway. Girls rolled up their skirts to create mini-skirts and boys either wore pointed 'winkle-picker' shoes ('winks') or 'chisels' with narrow square-cut toes. I never really took to winks, but chisels were good. In the fifth and sixth-form I began to wear my old Sea Cadet bell-bottoms to school too. Non-conformity was cool.

In my penultimate year at school, we 'A' level geography students went on a week-long field trip to the Lake District to study the effects of glacial erosion and so on. The expedition was led by the head of geography, George Walker and we stayed in a hostel called Newlands and, from there, hiked the valleys and fells. It was a great experience, but I had reached a certain age and I had had my eye on a pretty girl who was working at a coffee shop just down the valley. On the last day of our trip I plucked up the courage and arranged with her that I should sneak out of the hostel and meet her after she finished work.

Close by, there ran a mountain stream which happened to be very fast-flowing following heavy rain. Out of the hostel I duly sneaked and, being a few minutes early, hands in pockets, I began to hop casually from one riverside rock to another. It's amazing how slippery a rock can become when wet and, before I knew what had hit me, I was being rolled under the freezing water with my hands still firmly stuck in my pockets. I struggled and gulped, freed my hands, ripped my pockets and was bashed and scraped as I was funnelled under the little stone bridge. After what seemed like an age, I managed to drag myself out, gasping and spluttering onto the bank. Grazed, bruised and soaking wet, I hobbled back into the hostel to explain myself and to dry out. I never saw the girl again.

Eight

Hello Sailor!

As the austerity of the immediate post-war years began to ease, slowly but surely, families began to feel a little more prosperous. By the late fifties and into the sixties, going on an annual holiday became more commonplace. For many, it still meant simply fixing a roof rack on the old Austin A30, humping a couple of battered suitcases on top, covering them with a flapping waterproof sheet and heading for the nearest seaside. In our part of the world, this meant Cleethorpes, Skegness, Mablethorpe or one of the other small villages on the North Sea Coast. For anyone who has never been to this part of England's coastline, the North Sea is *not* the blue Mediterranean. It is mostly very cold, very brown and, until fairly recently, very polluted. Hence, it has been said that the unappetising prospect of swimming in the sea at Cleethorpes is not so much a question of swimming as 'going through the motions'.

Our first family holiday was in Robin Hood's Bay near Whitby on the North Yorkshire coast. I have no memory of it and my sister was only a baby, so it must have been in about 1953 or 1954 and the only accommodation my parents could afford was a converted railway carriage parked by the sea. Apparently, a good time was had by all, except for my sister, who fell out of a high chair onto her face..and that's all I know about my first holiday.

The journey to and from the seaside was often an adventure in itself because cars were pretty unreliable by today's standards. It was almost expected that there would be at least one break in the journey to repair a puncture, mend a fuel pump or tighten a fan belt. A journey of thirty or forty miles sometimes took half a day, so inevitably a stop at a roadside pub was a requirement. Whilst parents went in for a pint, the kids were left out in the car with packets of Smiths Crisps (complete with small twist of blue waxed paper containing salt) and maybe a bottle of Dandelion and Burdock or Tizer. Children were most definitely not welcome in public houses and, even though we had three pubs in our village, I don't think I set foot in one until I was at least fifteen years old.

For as long as I can remember, I have held a fascination for rivers, lakes and the sea. Maybe it's a throwback to distant Viking ancestors or maybe just thanks to my Mum's father, Grandad Ogden, who was a fisherman for many years, working on Grimsby trawlers, scouring the cold and dangerous seas off Iceland for cod. He showed me how to repair nets, using a skill that he called 'tatting' (although I have long since forgotten how to do it), whilst telling his salty tales. He had also spent some time working in a brewery and was given beer as part of his wages. Like many of his generation however, the one period he rarely spoke of, was the 1914-18 Great War, fighting in the trenches. He had a habit, when sitting doing nothing but thinking his own thoughts, of moving his right thumb in a rapid circular motion. It seems that he had been wounded in the Battle of Mons and spent time in a field hospital where his broken hand was repaired and a part of his recovery process involved physiotherapy and thus exercising his mended thumb. He must have been a very good patient because, as far as I know, he carried on with the exercise until the very end of his life. It might simply be that nobody told him to stop..

In about 1964, my parents decided to take a holiday on The Norfolk Broads, an idyllic area of wetlands, navigable rivers and lakes, which are in fact ancient flooded peat workings. The area is now a popular National Park but in the sixties it was still regarded as a fairly wild and remote place and was hence much quieter than it is today. They rented a waterside bungalow in Wroxham, a village on the River Bure, for a week and I still remember the smell of the black tar covering the little house which was reached down a narrow village lane. It was a simple bungalow with a small, neat lawn and a sagging black timber boathouse over a peaceful inlet off the main river. In the boathouse floated two small clinker-built wooden boats – one rigged for simply rowing and the other with a gaff-rigged sail, rudder and centre-board for bolder adventures.

My Dad was hooked.. and so, therefore, was I. We dabbled and splashed, fished and explored. We learned how to hoist the sail, read the wind and the current, we watched other boats, large and small, including magnificent wherries, the large sailing barges that have plied these East Anglian waters for centuries – and we marvelled. I was too young to know it then, but this short, happy period of time spent on the Norfolk Broads with my family and a little wooden boat, was the first manifestation of my ongoing love affair with the sea.

My parents were so captivated by the world of waterways, windmills and reed-beds that the following year they went a step further and hired a wooden six-berth motor cruiser named *Edith E*, featuring a sliding coach roof over a centre cockpit and a neat little open stern cockpit with gates for boarding a dinghy. We enjoyed ourselves so much, exploring the rivers and broads, that the following year we continued the adventure in another cruiser, *Rowan Chieftain*. I have few memories of these trips but there are loads of family photos showing happy children wearing life-jackets.

I do have a memory of a place called Potter Heigham, a small village on the banks of the River Thurne. There is a lovely brick and stone-built medieval bridge, believed to date from 1385, on a tidal stretch of the river. In those days, the local entertainment consisted of watching cruisers attempting to pass under the main arch of the bridge. This could only be attempted at low water and, even then, it was very tight. On one occasion, Dad recruited a dozen or so burley drinkers from the local pub to come aboard and weigh down our boat just enough to squeeze it through the arch on a rising tide. Cruisers have been stuck fast under it and many boat parts have been knocked off and skulls bashed by its stones. So much so that I understand that it is now compulsory to use a pilot to navigate any hire craft through the tricky arch.

When I was twelve or thirteen, I joined the Sea Cadet Corps in Lincoln. The unit, named *T.S. Wrangler*, was based in a couple of old wartime Nissen huts on the waterside at Brayford Pool to the south-west of the city centre. *T.S.* stands for *Training Ship* and the Sea Cadets had close links to the Royal Navy, using the same uniforms and following similar training programmes, often involving visits to active naval bases for gunnery training and so on. The Sea Scouts, in contrast, are part of the wider Scouting movement. I had developed an ambition to join the Royal Navy and the Sea Cadets provided a great introduction to general seamanship and other activities associated with life in the navy. My friend Nick Kennedy joined at the same time so we were able to travel in together by bus every Tuesday and Friday evening. We soon made new friends and took to it like ducks to water, learning how to take care of our uniforms, march in formation, do rifle drill, salute and blow a bosun's whistle.

We learned how to row and sail in ex-navy cutters and old clinker-built, twenty-seven-foot long 'whalers', each of which were typically crewed by five cadets. These were ex-Royal Navy boats that were designed to withstand the most severe sea and weather conditions and to be manned by naval boarding parties. The whalers in particular were very heavy wooden boats. They took some pulling and I can't think of those lovely traditional boats without recalling the soreness of fresh blisters on my hands. We learned how to tie bowlines and sheet-bends, make an eye-splice, how to send messages by semaphore, Morse code and signal flags and how to read nautical charts. I found it all fascinating and many of the skills learned then came in very useful later on in my life.

In our unit there was a small detachment of Royal Marine Cadets and, every so often, we would join in night exercises with them in the overgrown grounds of Sobraon Barracks in Lincoln. The barracks were, at that time only used by reservists, but had originally been home to the Royal Lincolnshire Regiment with whom my grandfathers had served during the First World War. We were divided into small groups and had to black our faces and creep about in the dark carrying heavy Lee Enfield .303 rifles and trying to reach certain objectives without being detected. This was great fun for young lads. We were also taught to shoot on the indoor range at the barracks.

Some of our officers had seen naval service in the Second World War and I remember a lieutenant telling stories of the Arctic convoys, taking vital supplies to Archangel and Murmansk in Russia. The conditions were such that ice built up so much on the superstructure and rigging that crews had to chip it away. It was so cold that, if you inadvertently touched any metal with your bare hands, the flesh would instantly freeze and stick so that tearing it away would leave raw skin on metal.

There was one eventful weekend when I took part in a Sea Cadet regatta in the port of Hartlepool in County Durham, on the north-east coast. We had to sail and row against rival crews from other parts of the U.K. and three of us travelled the 130 miles or so there in an old Morris Minor owned by seventeen-year old Maddison, the only one of us old enough to drive. As we arrived in the town, there suddenly appeared in front of us a man on a bike wearing a flat cap at a jaunty angle and clutching a huge bunch of flowers. The man was clearly very drunk and, with a magnificent wobble, he parted company with the bicycle and lay sprawled across the bonnet of our car, still clutching the lovely bunch of flowers. Maddison stamped the brake, the man slithered off, dusted himself down, retrieved his battered bike and wobbled off again into the sunset, apparently unharmed.

If that was our introduction to Hartlepool, unbeknown to us, there were more surprises to come. Having settled into our quarters, we were proudly wearing our uniforms and, despite being under-age, we decided to go to a local pub for a drink. We were still inexperienced young lads but we swaggered our way into the nearest 'local', bought our pints and stood at one end of the bar feeling quite pleased with ourselves. Slowly the pub became busier and noisier, filling up with a motley mix of fairly rough-looking characters and we found ourselves pressed into a corner.

Then there was a scuffle and some yelling and suddenly all hell broke loose. Bar stools were splintered, glasses were smashed and a man staggered past us with his nose split open by a broken bottle. There were shouts about somebody's woman and fists were flying in all directions. No sooner had the brawl got going nicely, than a shout went up, 'Look out, the bluebottles are coming!' The door flew open, whistles blew and, sure enough, half a dozen constables with a police dog ran in and began to set about the brawlers. Their response had been so swift that they must literally have been waiting round the corner for the trouble to start. Clearly, we hadn't chosen the most select part of town for our quiet drink but, miraculously, we had escaped the melée so, abandoning our half-finished pints, we clung to the walls and shimmied our way out of the scrum, heaving massive sighs of relief.

As far as the sailing and rowing was concerned, I don't think we won any trophies, but we did our best in unfamiliar surroundings. The weekend was not over yet however and the journey home turned out to be quite an experience. Three of us piled into Maddison's old Morris again and I was nicely settled in the back seat. I soon dozed off contentedly. It was pouring with rain and the windscreen wipers were barely able to cope with the spray as we drove along a duel-carriageway heading south. We were overtaking a big tanker truck when I was disturbed by a sudden change in the motion of the car. We had hit standing water and the car aquaplaned out of control and I opened my eyes to see on-coming traffic. Maddison managed to pull the car back on to the carriageway, narrowly missing the tanker but again he lost it and we found ourselves rolling down a steep embankment. I clearly remember thinking, 'This is where I die'. Bizarrely, everything was happening in slow motion as the adrenaline kicked in and I had time to think of curling into a ball, tucking my head down as I bumped in slow motion from floor to window to roof.

The car came to a rest upside-down after somersaulting through a wooden fence at the bottom of the embankment. I was alive. We were *all* alive. The engine was still racing and there was a smell of raw fuel. I heard breathless voices outside shouting and, within a few moments, we were out of the car, squatting, dazed and a little bruised, in long wet grass. Somebody cut the engine and I recall the police arriving. We must all have been in shock because we were shaking but, once they realised we weren't going to die, the policemen seemed more interested in the car, which they said was a complete write-off.

They arranged for a local garage to collect it later in the day and then, even more bizarrely, they drove off, leaving us to make our own way home. So it was that the three of us found ourselves standing with our kit-bags in the rain at the side of a dual-carriageway, with our thumbs shakily extended, hoping for a ride south. Before long, a blue Ford stopped and we piled in. The driver was a sales rep. and he babbled that he had to be in Coventry or somewhere by six or something and he slammed his toe to the floor. He drove - and talked - like a man possessed, but we were grateful to be heading homewards as fast as possible. Then, without warning, the brake-lights of a car ahead flashed on and..screech..Bang! We ran into the back of it.

In fact the collision was not serious and the two drivers must have sorted things out between themselves quickly, because we were soon on our way again, but you can imagine the effect of yet another crash on the already-shredded nerves of three young lads. When I eventually reached home, I said nothing to my parents of the pub brawl or the crashes for fear that I would not be allowed to go away again. In fact, I never did tell them, but I was certainly never so happy and relieved to return to the safe comforts of the family home.

In the spring of 1966 my Sea Cadet unit held a draw to choose 6 boys for a trip to Malta with the Royal Navy. My close friend Nick Kennedy won a place but, at the last minute, he caught the mumps and had to drop out. I was the next choice and so suddenly found myself heading with five others to Plymouth to join H.M.S. Hampshire, a County Class guided missile destroyer. These ships were the size of small battle cruisers and the Hampshire had only been operational for two or three years and so was pretty well a state-of-the-art warship, carrying, apart from guns, large Sea Slug missiles, smaller Sea Cat missiles and a Westland Wessex helicopter. It was powered by gas turbine engines and I remember the sound being similar to the jet engine of an aircraft as we moved away from port. Life on board was comfortable and we quickly slotted into the naval 'watch' system, joining the regular naval crews as they went about their work. I was only fifteen but some of the youngest sailors on board were only about a year older than me.

The food was excellent and we, along with the regular crew, were given a daily tot of rum from an ornate polished oak barrel marked, 'The Queen, God Bless Her'. This tradition was abolished in 1970. Certain parts of this very modern ship were secret and out-of-bounds to us and we were not allowed to take any photographs whilst on board. We were given supervised tours of the Operations Room, the heart of the ship which was bathed day and night in a pink-red light. Men wearing white flash hoods and headphones spoke in hushed tones and there were large transparent screens marked with the positions of Soviet submarines and other vessels of interest. To us it was very exciting in a 'James Bond' sort of way. I was also very impressed by the massive hangar-like missile magazine, stacked with weapons loaded with various types of warheads, ready to be hydraulically loaded onto the twin launchers at the stern of the ship.

I enjoyed watching the large Wessex helicopter landing on flight deck and being trundled into its hangar. The helicopter crews exercised most days, being sent off in all directions on various missions, practising submarine detection by dipping sonar devices into the sea whilst hovering and then reporting back to the ship. They were the extra eyes and ears of the ship, operating at great distances and providing invaluable intelligence. The ship typically cruised at around twenty-five knots (almost 30 m.p.h.) and I loved watching the helicopter hover alongside and then skilfully 'side-slipping' onto the deck, where crews then rushed out with straps and clips to secure it before the roll of a wave could send it over into the safety nets.

It's sometimes hard to appreciate the speed of these large warships. I was once told to join a team cleaning the anchor cable on the foc'sle (the pointy deck at the front). Imagine trying to stand on the roof of a car travelling at 30 m.p.h whilst wielding a broom and you come close. Add to that the fact that the metal deck is streaming with salt water and keeps pitching and rolling by ten or fifteen degrees and you begin to understand the problem. I have a sneaking feeling that cleaning the cable is one of those jobs reserved for green newcomers - and I decided I wanted to be a naval helicopter pilot.

When the *Hampshire* arrived in Valletta's Grand Harbour in Malta, the island still provided an active base for the British Royal Navy, even though the country had become independent from Britain in 1964. I remember that we had to 'man the deck' wearing No. 1 uniforms as we sailed into Valletta. Manning the deck on entering a foreign harbour is an ancient tradition designed to show that all men not actually on duty controlling the ship are not manning weapons and therefore the intention is purely peaceful. To be a part of that tradition as a powerful warship enters an ancient port does fill one with pride and I imagine that, still today, crowds gather on quaysides to watch the spectacle, as they have for many centuries.

Once ashore, we were billeted in the ancient Fort St. Angelo, or H.M.S. St. Angelo as it was also known. The place reeked of history and I remember our bunk-room had very thick stone walls and a slowly-turning electric fan hanging from the ceiling. The fort had withstood the Ottoman Turks during the Great Siege of Malta in 1565, thanks largely to the ingenuity and resilience of the Grand Master of the Christian Knights of Malta, Jean de Valette and his forces. They withstood a brutal onslaught orchestrated by the Sultan, Suleiman the Magnificent in which they were greatly out-numbered. There is a terrific account of this dramatic few months in a book by Ernle Bradford, *The Great Siege: Malta 1565,* in which he relates in great detail the sheer brutality and determination of the Ottoman Janissaries and the Christian Knights to possess this island as a vital staging post in the Mediterranean. Valletta is named after Jean de Valette, Grand master of the Order of Hospitallers (Knights of St. John of Jerusalem), who eventually prevailed over the Ottoman attackers.

We spent a few pleasurable days exploring from our fortress base, courtesy of the Royal Navy. We took the disas, or dghajas, traditional little wooden water-taxis to and from Birgu. At night, we were shown the seedy side of Valletta in Strait Street, known by British sailors as 'The Gut'. Girls would call out, offering their services and the drink flowed like water as the sailors spent all their pay. I remember naval patrols in No. 1 uniforms, wearing white gaiters and belts, armed with long truncheons, mopping up the drunks and policing the brawls. The street was notorious and packed from end to end with bars, brothels and music halls – quite an eye-opener for six young cadets, but as valuable a part of our education as the Latin and Geography of school. One hot afternoon we were taken sailing in small boats to explore the magnificent Grand Harbour whilst awaiting the arrival of the ship that would take us home.

The *Hampshire* had quietly sailed out of Malta and continued on her mission eastwards and so we embarked, as planned, onto *H.M.S. Lincoln*, an ageing Aircraft Direction Frigate. She was on her way back for de-commissioning in the U.K. after a tour of duty based in Singapore. We heard from members of her crew that they had seen action during anti-piracy patrols off the coast of Borneo and the ship and her crew were certainly more 'battle-hardened' than we had experienced before. The sailors were fit and tanned and ready for anything – especially a good night out down the Gut.

I was shown to a junior mess, known affectionately as 'The Jungle' down in the bowels of the ship where we slept in hammocks, just like the ones used in Nelson's 18th century navy. I understand that the *Lincoln* was the last active ship in the Royal Navy to use hammocks and I struggled to sleep in mine. Not only is climbing in and out of a swinging piece of canvas an acquired skill, but there is no choice other than sleeping on one's back and I was used to lying on my side. Hence I often found myself sleeping in a blanket on the steel floor underneath the mess table. The Jungle mess was reached by a vertical steel ladder and I have memories of drunk sailors falling down the ladder and landing with a thud and a curse, so the only safe place for me was under the table. The ship sailed from Malta to Gibraltar, where, during a tour of the rock in a navy Land Rover, I was jumped on by a pesky Barbary ape. We then continued towards Plymouth via the Bay of Biscay, where we experienced a severe storm.

Now and again, without warning, a ship's captain decides that the crew must practise 'Man Overboard Drill' and, naturally, there is little point in doing this in a flat calm. Generally, if someone decides to fall overboard, they don't choose a lovely balmy day to do it, they lurch over the rail in the pouring rain in a force ten storm featuring thirty or forty-foot-high waves. I heard the shrill notes of an alarm and urgent commands being shouted over a loudspeaker. Something like, 'Man overboard! Man overboard! Hands to Stations! Hands to Stations!' Next, I felt a sharp tap on my shoulder and a burly Petty Officer said, 'You, lad – Boat crew. Get in the boat!' Hence I found myself in a wildly swinging ship's lifeboat with four or five men, fumbling with oil-skins and a life-jacket whilst trying to hang on for all I'm worth.

In an emergency, a warship is not able to stop quickly so the quickest way of returning to the point where a man has fallen into the sea is to execute a huge loop. In the meantime, a boat is launched as fast as possible from the moving ship to pick up the 'person' (in this practice situation, a flotation dummy). Our boat was thus dangled from its' davits, or hoisting cranes, as the fast-moving ship heaved and plunged in the grey waves. The release of the boat from the ship requires great skill. We were banging against the side of the ship. The inboard engine of the boat was running, the rudder held hard over and the coxswain waited for us to be dropped onto a suitable wave. He snapped a shackle and, bang – we hit the water running, immediately steering away from the ship as fast as possible to avoid damage. To describe the process as a roller-coaster ride is to greatly under-state it. It was simply unbelievably frightening and there was more to come.

If the launch was scary, we then had to head back to the last known position of the dummy in a very small boat, riding 30-foot waves and plunging into 30-foot troughs. One moment you are balanced precariously looking at only sky and the next you are in a very deep liquid hole with mountains of cold water seemingly about to devour you. All I could do was hang on hard to the thwart of the lifeboat to avoid being thrown over the side and then I realised that the ship had now left us behind and we were in a speck of a boat being churned in a maelstrom of salt water and spray.

Having successfully 'rescued' our casualty, it seemed like an eternity before the grey bulk of the ship re-appeared and we had to go alongside in the same wild conditions to be hooked up again. I remember life-lines being dropped and we were instructed to climb up and so, shaking like a leaf, I found myself climbing hand-over-hand up the slippery side of a rolling warship. When you watch swash-buckling pirates in the movies, swarming up the sides of Spanish galleons, it all looks so easy but, believe me, it is not. I was more than ready for a sit down and a hot drink when I arrived back in the 'Jungle'.

During the following hours the storm abated and, since the ship was returning to Plymouth for decommissioning, it was decided that there would be some weapons training to use up some ammunition. Thus the ship began to slowly circle, a couple of empty oil drums were dumped overboard to act as targets and we were instructed in firing heavy machine guns and sten guns until we sank them. A parachute flare was then fired high into the air and we took turns on the 45mm Bofors anti-aircraft guns to try to bring it down. The ship also featured a triple-barrelled anti-submarine mortar weapon called *Squid* which fired 300mm diameter bombs right over the top and ahead of the advancing ship. Like depth-charges, they exploded in patterns and at pre-set depths to kill submarines and it was exciting for us to see the towering plumes of water directly ahead as the weapons detonated.

All of this excitement was great but, when it was all over, I realised that I had gone completely deaf. The navy had neglected to provide me with any ear protection and I could hear virtually nothing for several days. I was only fifteen and it worried me that I may hear nothing for the rest of my life but, eventually, my hearing recovered - although I still suffer from tinnitus to this day, thanks to the Royal Navy.

The three-week experience of naval life reinforced my desire to join up, so I applied for officer training at Britannia Royal Naval College in Dartmouth on the South Devon coast. To my surprise, I was invited to attend the Admiralty Interview Board at H.M.S. Sultan in Gosport where I had to stay overnight. After being collected from the station by a chauffeur-driven car, treated to a dinner with full silver-service and an introductory talk, all candidates were submitted to a day and a half of 'grilling' by naval officers, education experts and so on. There were also physical tests in the gym and tests of leadership potential involving, for instance, small teams crossing a mock river without 'falling in'.

To my amazement, I was told that I had passed and would be accepted into Dartmouth subject to passing my 'O 'level exams and also my 'A' levels at age eighteen. Acceptance also depended on passing a thorough medical examination in London. I was still only sixteen and, as far as I was concerned, filled with the certain knowledge that I was indestructible. As far as I could see my future was now wonderfully certain and I would be cruising effortlessly through the rest of my schooling and then on into the glamorous life of a globe-trotting officer and gentleman.

Except it was not to be. When it came to the medical tests, it was found that the hearing in my left ear was not quite up to scratch. After some humming and haa-ing, this was overlooked when I explained that the problem had in fact resulted from naval gunfire. The eye tests were exhaustive, involving, as well as the usual squinting at charts and tweaking with an assortment of amusing lenses, sitting in a completely dark room straining to spot tiny pinpoints of coloured light.

It was discovered that, although my vision was fine, I had a form of hypertropia or slight vertical misalignment in my eyes. Until then, I had been blissfully unaware of the problem but, as far as the navy was concerned, I would be rejected. It was explained to me that I might opt to have surgery, which might or might not solve the problem, but then I would have to re-apply to join the Royal Navy and there was no guarantee that I would be even invited to an interview the next time round, let alone be accepted. I hated the idea of messing with a pair of eyeballs that were apparently doing a pretty good job and decided that a life as a Royal Navy helicopter pilot was clearly not meant to be. The dream was over..

Nine

Drum and Bass

In the mid sixties, four school friends ganged together to form a little jazz group called 'The Richard Adrian Quartet'. The name came from the three founding members, all of whom had middle names of either Richard or Adrian. I joined later and my middle name is John but we all thought the name sounded cool, so we stuck with it, sometimes abbreviating it to RAQ. The core talent was provided by my good friend Phil Parker on piano and Nick Bankes on double bass. Kevin Curley, played clarinet and I pitched in later to complete the quartet on drums. We were all aged fifteen and sixteen.

Phil was a child prodigy, a natural musician who had reached high grades in Royal School of Music exams on piano, but who was equally at home playing acoustic guitar, trombone, mandolin and bass. His talents were not confined to music though and he excelled in all sciences, subsequently going on to gain a PhD in Applied Physics, amongst other qualifications. Initially, I had no proper drum kit, so I cobbled one together from a few borrowed cymbals, a snare drum from the school music department and a massive bass drum from the Sea Cadets that had been used by a marching band. It was a while before I managed to afford a real kit in sparkling pearlescent white.

In true 'jack-of-all-trades' fashion, I had experimented with a few different instruments, including the flute, trumpet and guitar and, whilst I loved the idea of being able to play, I had never settled into the hard grind of really learning. Dad once bought me an ancient banjo from an auction but again, I just plonked around with it, always being distracted by other activities including sailing with the Sea Cadets. Nevertheless, I had always enjoyed music from my days with the church choir and, by the time I was fifteen I was, in common with most kids, really into the music of the Beatles and other up-and-coming sixties groups.

Being in a band was great and we all threw ourselves into it with the energy and careless confidence of youth. We would practise whenever possible, sometimes getting ourselves into trouble with teachers. There was a music room in our school with two or three tiny practice cubicles, each of which had a piano in it and space for little else. At every opportunity, all four of us would be crammed in there with sheet music, double bass, clarinet and perhaps just a snare drum for good measure. Despite these rooms being sound-proofed, we would kick up such a noise that complaints were common.

Our bass player Nick's father, Monty Bankes, was our French teacher and he had once been an orchestral double bass player. I believe that, during the war, he had worked for British Intelligence with some kind of French connection and I could imagine him being flown in to liaise with the Resistance. He was small, quick-witted, a fluent French speaker and, as well as teaching his son to play the bass, had a talent for drama and music production. He gave us invaluable advice on how to bring expression into our music, interpret mood and so on. Through him, we became interested in the work of jazz musicians like Jacques Loussier, Ramsey Lewis and Dave Brubeck and soon Phil, with Monty's help would even arrange pieces by Bach into a jazz format.

Initially we played nervously at school concerts but, as our confidence and our repertoire grew, we began to play small pub gigs and at a few parties in village halls. We were able to cover a cross-section of musical genres so would be equally happy banging out 'When I'm Sixty-Four' by the Beatles, 'Sunny Afternoon', by The Kinks, 'Unsquare Dance', by Dave Brubeck or 'The Blue Danube' waltz by Strauss. We played a cabaret evening at The Raven Club, R.A.F. Waddington in January 1970 and I recently found a note proudly stating, 'I received £7.2s.0d for about ¾ hour playing'. It sounds like a pittance now, but a student would only expect to earn £12 to £15 per *week* for casual work in those days.

Transport was always a problem but Monty Bankes helped us in the early days, ferrying us to and fro' in his estate car to Friday and Saturday night bashes. His son, Nick, was a little more than a year older than the rest of us so, when he was seventeen, he quickly passed his driving test and was allowed to borrow the car. Much later, as we acquired cars at age seventeen, we managed to pile our equipment into them and thus became self-sufficient. It would seemingly be impossible to cram a double bass into one of the old Ford Populars, but with great ingenuity, Nick Bankes managed it, albeit with the long neck and head sticking out of the window. One weekend, we entered a talent contest at Skegness, playing a couple of Beatle numbers. We came first, but the prize was a weekend for two in Amsterdam, so we sold it on and shared the cash.

It was 1967 before I began to drive on the open road at the age of sixteen. My dad bought me an old red and white AC Petite three-wheeler car which I was able to drive on a provisional licence, just like a motorcycle. I'm not saying I was ungrateful because it was my first means of powered transport, but those three-wheelers weren't exactly babe magnets, bearing as they did, a close resemblance to invalid cars. It had an uncomfortable bench seat, was made chiefly of aluminium and so was very light and it felt flimsy, as if it would blow over in a strong breeze. The three wheels were small and so every bump and rut in the road sent judders up the spine. It was powered by a very noisy Villiers engine and, as I remember, had no reverse gear but it would turn in its own length. In retrospect, I guess my dad bought it in cahoots with my mum to avoid the possibility that I would be tempted onto a motorcycle with all the perceived danger that entailed. I remember the engine screaming like a banshee as the poor thing strained to carry me up Waddington Hill and, even now, I feel the embarrassment.

Meanwhile, at school, we continued to use every spare moment to practise our music. Phil lived with his parents in a bungalow only about a five minute walk from the school gates and it was not unknown for us to sneak out, nip round to his place and do a half-hour practice session. There were even a couple of times when we set off on cross-country runs only to make a swift left turn to his door, thrash out some tunes for a while and then, having daubed ourselves with a little dirt, straggle back through the school gates, panting theatrically.

I managed to find a booking agent who agreed to take us on and, from then on, the gigs became more frequent and varied. We played at the Geest Bananas Social Club out in the Lincolnshire fens near Spalding where women old enough to be our mothers did rude things on the dance floor. We played cabaret evenings and once backed a magician with dramatic crescendos and drum-rolls as he poured a pint of beer into a rolled-up newspaper, only to unroll the perfectly dry paper, re-roll it and pour the beer back into the glass. I was drumming only a few feet behind the man and I couldn't see how he did it. We played at village hall dances; everything from rumbas and foxtrots to Manfred Mann. It was great fun and, even after we left school and all went our different ways to universities and colleges, whenever we were home, we re-united to earn a few pounds.

On Christmas Eve 1970, we were booked by our enthusiastic agent, to play in Boston at a large popular music venue called *The Gliderdrome*. I was nervous about this because the place was way out of our league, having featured artists like Jimi Hendrix, Ike and Tina Turner, Procol Harum, Status Quo and Stevie Wonder. Now The Richard Adrian Quartet was in the line-up and I was seriously worried that our agent had all but signed our death warrant. But we needed the money.

Fortunately, we were not the main act, but merely there to keep the show going while the main act, a deafening rock band, took a break. It was snowing like hell and we struggled to arrive on time, battling the icy conditions in our pathetic trio of bangers loaded with our very basic equipment. We appeared on, what was to us, a massive stage in front of a seething mass of drunk bikers and their molls. It was almost as frightening as being launched over the side of a warship in a force ten storm, but once we began to play, the crowd, in their state of generous inebriation, apparently forgave us and we got away with it by the skin of our teeth. We had the presence of mind to realise that we had to make a joke of it. It was Christmas, so we just played silly tunes like 'Rudolph the Red-Nosed Reindeer' as fast and furiously as we could and it seemed to do the trick. When I think back to those times, I have to remind myself of just how young we were when we started, in many cases not even legally old enough to be allowed through the door of the pubs and clubs in which we played.

Ten

Vive la Différence

Back in the summer of 1960, Mum and Dad had bought a nice big frame tent with an awning and had packed it, along with everything but the kitchen sink, into the family car for a holiday in south Devon. I don't remember if it was for one week or two, but I do know that, from the moment we arrived there, to returning home, it rained and rained and rained. The campsite, somewhere near Torquay, was nothing but a quagmire and a farm tractor was summoned to pull caravans to and fro' covered in gloopy mud. It was more like trench warfare than a holiday. We were so fed up with the relentless biblical deluge as we crouched shivering over playing cards in a soggy tent, that we decided a holiday in warmer climes was a must for the following summer.

The old Vauxhall Velox that we had taken on the ill-fated Devon trip the previous year was a little past its best. Dad had shared it with Ray Blades and, on one occasion, rounding a sharp corner in Bracebridge Heath, the rear passenger door had flown open and my younger brother Fred had been thrown clean out onto the tarmac. Fortunately, he had only suffered a broken arm, but it might easily have been so much worse. Dad had therefore invested in a nice second-hand Ford Zodiac which would be perfect for transporting a family and camping equipment through France. We fitted a roof rack and, when the time came, strapped on our trusty home-made kayak, painted the headlights yellow, stuck a GB sticker on the back and set off for our first foreign holiday.

Making our way through rural France was a pure delight. There were no motorways and the main route south was the famous Route N7. Although, by today's standards, it was not crowded, there were plenty of heavy trucks as well as holiday traffic and Dad decided that, where practical, we would take a less direct route on the minor 'D' roads to experience *La France Profonde*. We had rarely seen cars like Panhards, Peugeots, little Renault Fours and the ubiquitous Citroen 2CVs and we noticed that even the olive-skinned school children in villages were confidently whizzing around on Solex motorised bikes and Mobylettes, with baguettes clutched under their arms. We stopped and browsed in outdoor markets and, as we headed further south, there were roadside stalls selling melons and peaches or nougat. I don't think I had ever before tasted a peach that didn't come from a tin and I couldn't believe how succulent they were, with juice that poured down my chin.

Like most British people at the time, we were amused and a tad disgusted by the public flush toilets that were simply 'holes in the ground' with ceramic foot pads where you crouched, sometimes gripping onto grab handles for support. Mum once went to use one of these on a campsite, only to be surprised when an indignant toad jumped out of the hole underneath her.

In those days, so much about France was different from the U.K. As we passed through the countryside during that first visit, we saw few tractors but plenty of working horses and even a few oxen pulling their wooden carts. Further south there were neat vineyards, fields of sunflowers, tobacco, maize and melons, all of which were completely new to us. We practised our French as we bought our bread, cheese and patisseries and we tried olives and olive oil for the first time. In England, olive oil was purely medicinal – for putting a few drops in your ear if you had an ache – whereas, in France, it was for cooking, making a dressing, or simply dipping bread in. We all revelled in the relaxed atmosphere, the food, the scenery and the sunshine – and so began a love of that country.

Having settled in at the campsite by the Mediterranean, we couldn't help comparing it to the seaside beaches of The North Sea in our native Lincolnshire. It was warm and calm and blue. Swimming was a pleasure and we learned to use snorkels and chase after fish. We paddled our kayak and soaked up the sun, played beach games and quenched our thirsts with Orangina or lemonade from heavy glass flip-top bottles. Beach-sellers would stroll along selling sweet-coated roasted nuts and women sun-bathed topless, or even naked if they felt like it. It was a different world. It felt like freedom - and we loved it.

We paid a few visits to St. Tropez, which had become a magnet for the rich and famous, thanks to the pouting film star, Brigitte Bardot and her cohort. We were captivated by the expensive yachts in the harbour, the restaurants, locals playing pétanque in the tree-lined square and artists selling their paintings on the quayside. In those days, St. Tropez was charming and very lively, but still welcoming. That summer was a real turning point in my life because, thanks to the misery of the Devon expedition, my parents had scrimped and saved to take us further afield. We therefore realised that there was a perfectly accessible world beyond England, waiting to be explored.

Having become hooked on continental holidays, the family sallied forth for a few weeks each summer for the next few years, heading to the South of France and also, once or twice, on to Spain. In those days, Spain was a very different place, still under the control of General Franco. Along the beaches around Tarragona there were, at intervals, sentry posts marked *Todo por la Patria* and manned by unfriendly armed officers of the feared Guardia Civil.

One particular year, back in France, there was one very sad experience by the sea. My brother Fred was snorkelling about 30 metres from the beach, when he spotted a young man seemingly snorkelling four or five metres down below him. He was marvelling at how he could hold his breath so well, when the boy slowly rolled over and he realised that something was very wrong. He raised the alarm and lots of people came to help. My father and a few others managed to pull him from the water but, despite the efforts of a doctor, the poor lad could not be revived. It shook all of us, not least Fred and we heard later that the casualty had had a heart condition, which was rare in such a young person and had suffered a catastrophic cardiac arrest whilst diving.

On a happier note, I remember once being on a campsite not far from Cannes from where we walked down to the beach one night and were surrounded by hundreds of thousands of fireflies glowing in the warm darkness. The spectacle is firmly etched in my memory and I have never seen a single firefly or glow-worm since that night.

Before long, I was at that awkward age when I did not want to go on holiday with my family. I didn't really even want to be seen with them and I must have been a total pain. That said, on June 25th in 1967, I found myself on what would be my final family holiday, in a crowded beach bar at the *Toison d'Or* (Golden Fleece) campsite, peering at a T.V. set that had been set up for a special event. It was the first ever live global satellite link-up of twenty five nations, reaching four hundred million people. For me, and most of the younger people present, the main attraction was The Beatles singing 'All You Need is Love' in real time, live from London. The song was written especially for the occasion with the aim of bringing the world together. It is hard to imagine now, in our age of mobile devices and instant worldwide visual communication, what it meant then to see real time broadcasts from all around the globe.

For my seventeenth birthday I was given a Morris Minor car. These were affectionately known as 'Moggie Minors' and my father had bought this particular one for £50 from a government auction at Ruddington near Nottingham where surplus military vehicles and equipment were sold to the public. The car had been adapted for use by disabled people, it was black and fitted with hand controls and was very low-mileage. Dad easily removed the hand controls and, to my delight, sprayed it bright red. Very soon, I passed my driving test and, within a couple of weeks, was heading off in the red Moggie with Nick Bankes, to the South of France for the summer. It occurred to me in later years that I might have, in all innocence, been driving illegally in France, being only seventeen. The minimum driving age in most of continental Europe at that time, was eighteen. The car was overloaded with a tent, camping and cooking gear and all kinds of stuff necessary for a couple of months of wandering. Whenever possible we would camp in farmers' fields for free.

We were both studying for our 'A' levels and we tried to practise our French as much as possible. We also made a point of visiting a few historic towns like Avignon, Nimes and Arles. In Orange, we went into the amazing Roman theatre, where productions and concerts are still staged. It is one of the best preserved Roman theatres in the world and I remember climbing to the very top of the terraced stone seating which forms a massive semi-circle. Nick stood in blazing sun on the stage far below, dominated by a white marble statue of Emperor Augustus. He spoke a few lines from

Le Bourgeois Gentilhomme by Molière, a play we were studying at school. The acoustics were so good that he hardly had to raise his voice for me to hear him perfectly clearly. The theatre dates back to the early 1st century A.D. and seats up to 7,000 people, all with a perfect view of the stage.

Another memorable sight was Le Pont du Gard, a 1st century Roman aqueduct bridge consisting of three tiers and crossing the deep valley of the River Gardon. It is a magnificent feat of engineering and was built as part of a 50 km long aqueduct delivering fresh water to the city of Nimes. In the sixties, although it had long been a tourist attraction, there were no facilities. We parked nearby and were able to walk right along the very top of its 275 metre length, some 48 metres (160 ft) above the valley below. The main water channel was capped by huge rectangular stones weighing five or six tons. These were missing in places and we could hop down to walk in the ancient water channel. The whole site was deserted and we were free to roam at will. Like the theatre in Orange, it is now a UNESCO World Heritage Site.

We always carried emergency rations from the U.K. in the car, not least in the form of Vesta Curries. These were ready meals and, although they were pretty awful, they were easy to prepare on a little gas stove. There was also the added benefit that the packet could double as a postcard. I never wanted to waste money buying cards so I sent scrawled updates every so often to my family on the back of a card proclaiming 'Vesta Beef Curry – This Meal is Simple and Quick' featuring a picture of brown gunge on rice.

Generally, during our travels, we lived in our little tent but sometimes, if we decided on a quick overnight stop, we slept in the car. The tiny Moggie Minor did not have reclining seats so we developed a special procedure for making ourselves comfortable. Firstly, we pulled out the back of the rear seat and stowed it underneath the car. This revealed an opening into the small boot. We then inflated two air mattresses which we wedged from the folded front seats to the rear of the car, protruding from the open boot. We then climbed into our sleeping bags and were able to lie with our feet sticking out of the car boot.

It was quite a performance and very cramped, but still quicker than pitching a tent. When the summer came to an end and it was time to head home, we left it until the last possible day and then drove like crazy the whole length of France in one go. We left very early in the morning to be sure of making Calais late at night for the cross-channel ferry. Remember, there were no motorways and the poor little car only had a maximum realistic speed of about 60 m.p.h. In short, we thrashed it as much as we dared and eventually arrived, after the crossing, in a drizzly Dover in the very early hours of the following morning in pitch darkness. We were desperately tired and quickly found somewhere to park in an open space. Our well-practised drill kicked in; pulling out back seat of car, blowing li-los, stripping to pants, car-boot open, sleeping bags poking out and zzzzzs.

At about 7 a.m., we were aware of noise and activity and, squeaking the condensation from the inside of the windows, saw to our horror that we were in the middle of a busy market. Stalls were already erected around us, goods were being laid out on trestle tables and we were surrounded by vans and the first customers of the day haggling over purchases. We dragged ourselves awake, dressed as quickly as possible, packed and started the car and then had to negotiate our way out through the throng. Apparently, the first arrivals had tried to wake us at around 5 a.m., but we were dead to the world and they had decided to let us sleep.

It must have been in 1969 when, on yet another leisurely summer of exploration, this time with my good friend Nick Kennedy, we found ourselves gloriously lost somewhere in the middle of rural

France. It was nearing dusk, so we took a random right turn off the road onto a very basic track heading goodness knows where. We soon came across an ancient couple, both dressed in black, topped by well-worn straw hats and walking slowly homeward. We drew to a dusty stop alongside them and, after the usual greetings, asked if they knew where it would be alright for us to camp for the night. The old man asked where we were from and we explained that we had driven from England. I had a can of English beer and a pack of biscuits in the car and I gave these to the couple, whereupon they both began to shed tears. We were just a couple of long-haired youths, but they explained that we were the first English men they had seen since the Second World War. I have no idea what memories the encounter stirred in these people, but it seemed likely they had suffered greatly back then, as did so many of their compatriots.

They said that we would be welcome to pitch our tent in one of their fields but that we should continue along the road to the family farm where we would find their son. This we did and, sure enough, the farmer was busy milking a bunch of placid brown cows in an old stone-built dairy across a cobbled courtyard. We said we had met his parents and he promptly directed us to a particular field with a solitary tree growing in the middle. There we gratefully pitched camp and began to cook, probably a Vesta beef curry, on our little gas stove.

We hung a lamp on the tree and were settling in nicely when a small procession approached across the meadow. The whole family, consisting of the now familiar grandparents, the farmer, his wife and a couple of children came and sat with us. They had brought bread, wine, cheese and other treats and we sat for hours discussing the world, the universe and everything. We felt as though we had landed from another planet. They were clearly intrigued by us and we, in turn, felt privileged and happy to spend time with these kind and gentle people.

Eleven

Dreams and Reality

The year was 1969. In April Robin Knox-Johnston had become the first man to sail non-stop around the world and, on the 20th of July, the first moon landing had taken place. It was also time for me to leave home and take my own 'small step' into the future, although it wasn't quite as momentous as that taken by Neil Armstrong. I was still hurting from the disappointment of being rejected by the Royal Navy and having nagging doubts about whether I should have opted for eye surgery to allow me to re-apply. I had set my heart on being a naval pilot and now had no idea what I wanted instead. I had half-heartedly gone through the motions of applying to a few universities but, despite passing all my 'O' and 'A' levels with good grades, none had accepted me. I had, however, been offered a place at the City of Leicester Polytechnic to do an H.N.D. in Business Studies.

I was eighteen years old and I threw myself into student life without really knowing why I was there. The course-work was fine and I decided to specialise in French and Marketing so, as well as the core subjects, Accounting, Business Law, and so on, I reasoned that Marketing might prove useful if I ever started my own business and the French course was very practical, teaching how to write job applications, invoices and the like.

I suspect that most students, me included, mainly have memories of the non-academic side of life away from home and family. My first student digs were down a scruffy back street in a house shared with five or six others and presided over by a slattern of a landlady called Jan and her lazy husband, Roy. I don't think she *meant* any harm, but our weekly rent of £2.10s included daily breakfast and an evening meal and the food was, quite frankly, revolting. She was the proud owner of a deep fat fryer and her culinary expertise was almost entirely limited to tossing anything and everything into its murky depths.

The handbook for a deep fat fryer, I feel sure, would recommend that the fat or oil should be changed now and again, but I suspect that Jan hadn't read it. Her meatballs would taste of cheese and a banana fritter would easily pass for a fish-cake. Whilst we were a pretty easy-going, resilient bunch of student residents, we soon reached the point where we feared for our health. We had raised our objections as politely as possible but still the torture continued, so direct action was urgently needed.

There used to be a product on the market called Bono Mint which was a very powerful laxative in the form of a gum. It happened to look and taste identical to a regular Beech Nut chewing gum, so we carefully made a switch and Jan was cleverly lured into accepting a packet. We saw nothing of her for the next three or four days. When she eventually did re-appear, she was a mere shadow of her former self. I don't remember if the food improved - and nothing was said, but hopefully she made a connection with her deep fat cooking and thought a little more about hygiene. I fear that the memory has left me with a deep-seated suspicion of fondues and what might be fished out of the bubbling pot. When I think of meal-times in that house, I'm reminded of a short verse by the great Spike Milligan:

A thousand hairy savages
Sitting down to lunch
Gobble gobble, glup glup
Munch munch munch

Luckily for me, my family home was only forty-odd miles away so, now and again, I would hitch-hike along the A46 to re-fuel on my mum's home cooking for a weekend. Hitching became an art-form and I learned very quickly about making eye-contact with drivers and trying to look 'respectable' to increase the chance of a free ride. Looking respectable went totally against the grain at that age and most students found that jumble sales and second-hand shops yielded some pretty bizarre garb. We were able to buy loon pants on Leicester Market for thirty shillings (£1.50) a pair in any colour from bright red to lemon yellow. These were tight cotton hipster trousers with twenty-four-inch flares. They sat *very* low on the hip and, when I say they were tight round the crotch, I mean they seriously affected the way we walked. I have no idea where I found them but I also remember for a while wearing a lovely pair of tight, deep red velour dungarees with huge flairs. Add to these a nice pair of platform boots, a stripy cheesecloth shirt, shoulder-length hair and you have the picture.

Things became unbearable for me at the house in Leicester when I found myself sharing a room with a poor guy who was schizophrenic. He would shout and scream in the night and suddenly jump out of bed, banging furniture and hitting the wall with his fists. Whilst I felt sympathetic and I tried to calm him, it was a hopeless situation. I couldn't sleep and I decided to leave. Other students in the house were also unhappy so we found rooms in a rented house on the other side of town where we could live without being at the mercy of live-in landlords.

This worked out pretty well and I shared my new room with a really easy-going engineering student called Terry. He was softly-spoken, with a strong Brummie accent, a very dry sense of humour and a mop of long brown hair. He was a perfect companion with one exception. I found myself waking up at night to a rasping, grating sound. For ages I just could not fathom what it was and I used to lie there, worried that we had a rat in the room. I mentioned it to Terry, but he said that he had heard no such thing and I must be dreaming. After some time, I realised that the sound came from Terry. He was a nocturnal teeth-grinder and, boy, was he good at it! He was blissfully unaware of the habit but I would be very surprised that, if he is still alive, he has anything but stumps left in his mouth.

I have the impression that today's students pay a little more attention to their health, but we lived on the cheapest food possible and I don't remember ever buying fresh fruit and vegetables. The only exception to this would be when we made huge communal pots of home-made soup or stew which we shared over a few days. I had a friend studying law who lived in a tiny bed-sit and, in the absence of a cooker, he heated up cans of baked beans on an upturned iron. Now and again, we would treat ourselves to egg, chips and peas in a local café for the grand price of 3s 6d (17½p). Luxury.

The top floor of the house was occupied by a mysterious group of students who never seemed to leave their domain. Most of the time, they kept themselves to themselves and you would hardly know they were in the building. However, now and again they would do crazy things like jumping out of the upstairs window into the gravel yard below. We learned that they experimented with, amongst other substances, L.S.D. which explained the occasional erratic behaviour. For reasons unknown, they would sometimes throw away their clothes and I found one or two nice pairs of jeans in the dustbins that fitted perfectly.

One of the other student occupants, Taffy, was a huge, bespectacled prop forward of a Welshman who lived in the next door room. He, Terry and I all had similarly eclectic tastes in music and we would sometimes stay up all night listening to Pink Floyd, Neil Young, Yes, Genesis, Santana, John Lee Hooker, Charlie Parker and anything else we could lay our ears on. Visits to pubs were rare, simply because we couldn't generally afford it, but the Student's Union events and house parties certainly kept us entertained. During 'Rag Week', the leaders of the Student's Union would organise, apart from the usual silly raft races and stuff, a 'Drink a Pub Dry' event.

There were 13,000 students in Leicester at the time and a pub would be selected as a target. I understand that the student fund-raising leaders would do a 'deal' with the landlord that the pub would literally be 'drunk dry' in one night in exchange for a percentage to go to charity. It all had to be arranged at the last minute to prevent a landlord getting wind of it and buying in a ridiculous volume of stock, but it was a no-brainer for the landlord and a very enjoyable challenge for the students. There was also an 'Eat a Fish-and-Chip-Shop Out' event which was just as successful, where every single fish, chip, mushy pea and pickled egg would be sold and devoured.

Basically, we spent all our spare time chasing after girls or listening to bands and there was plenty of scope for both. Every week we listened to bands like Free, The Terry Reid Band, Fairport Convention, The Strawbs with Rick Wakeman and loads of others, but the highlight of the student calendar was the Arts Ball, held at Leicester's Top Rank Suite. I seem to remember it being called 'The Groupies Ball'. A gang of us managed to obtain tickets for one of these events and I remember the line-up consisted of Spirit, a Californian band, Mott The Hoople, Joe Cocker and the Grease Band and The Bonzo Dog Band. It really was a wild event but, as far as I was concerned, the Bonzos were the most outstanding performers. Their mixture of comedy, psychedelic rock, jazz and sheer musicianship set them apart. Their founder member, Viv Stanshall, was in his prime and the entire set, featuring a bubble-blowing robot and Legs Larry Smith playing a musical leg, was pure pleasure. The Bonzos were highly talented musicians who really knew how to experiment, amuse and entertain. I still think they're great.

Twelve

Back to the Farm

My French lecturer at the Polytechnic was a tall, bespectacled academic called Bob Hope. In my second year, I discussed with him the possibility of spending the summer working in France to gain practical language experience. He promised to try help and, sure enough, he put me in touch with a French girl who was working in Leicester as a teacher. Her name was Sylviane and, when I met her over coffee, she explained that she came from a very small town in the department of Aveyron in the south. She knew a friendly local farming family who, she felt certain, would be happy to take on an extra pair of hands for the summer and so letters were exchanged and it was settled. I would live with the family on the farm for a few weeks and would be fed and accommodated in exchange for work.

At the end of the college term, I headed home to Waddington and began to prepare for my adventure. The little red Morris had to be dusted down, serviced and checked ready for a long drive. I worked as a driver for Dad for a week or two to earn a few pounds and met up with my old band mates to do a couple of sessions, all to help fund the trip. Before I knew it, Mum was fussing about, reminding me to write and not to drive too fast – and I was on my way south.

It felt strangely exhilarating to be heading off abroad alone, especially to stay in a house full of strangers who spoke no English. Would they be friendly? Would they work me to death? Would the beds be full of fleas? All of these questions and more flashed through my mind as I pushed on, made the ferry crossing to Dieppe and tried to cover some distance before pitching my tent for the night.

It was good to be driving through the French countryside again. I felt quite at home and, as on previous visits, I enjoyed the peacefulness and the familiar lush, green emptiness of it all. Towards dusk, somewhere deep in Normandy, I found a wide verge at the bottom of a field embankment just off a tiny side-road and I pitched my tent for the night. It was very quiet, apart from the croaking of distant frogs and a few birds wishing each other goodnight as I munched my bread and cheese.

I realised, as I settled into my sleeping bag, that I had never slept in a tent on my own before. I hadn't appreciated just how tired I was and so, before I knew it, I was sound asleep. SNORT, SNORT - GRUFFLE, SCRATCH, SNUFFLE!..I was instantly awake and paralysed. There was definitely something showing interest in my tent and it wasn't small. I felt a guy-rope twang and then a silent pause..then more snuffling. I thought of shining my torch out through the canvas to frighten whatever it was away, but I decided that, on balance it might make the intruder more curious, so I remained totally still, holding my breath. After what seemed an age, the creature shuffled off and I was left in peace. I never knew the nature of the beast – fox, badger, boar, stray dog or deer – because there was no sign the next day. However, the mind works overtime in these situations and I had nocturnal visions of woolly mammoths, escaped lunatics and yeti prowling in search of a solitary victim - and I never slept another wink that first night.

As usual, I stuck to minor roads and had an enjoyable drive throughout the next day, taking my time and stopping whenever I felt like it, in little villages or by streams, for a snack. That night, I parked up somewhere just south of Bourganeuf. I drank a whole bottle of cheap wine, feasted on supplies provided by my mother and fell into a deep sleep in the car. The farm I was heading for was home to the Cavaignac family, located in a tiny hamlet a short distance from Monbazens, a small town of about a thousand souls. The farming hamlet was not on the map and it took some finding, but at last I drove up to the front of an old stone farmhouse. It had a slate roof and sat prettily, surrounded by a few outbuildings, in a gentle green valley.

As I climbed stiffly from the little red car, a big rusty dog bounded towards me, barking like a crazy thing. I was used to dogs and wouldn't usually be worried by a charging hound, but I'd heard stories about farm dogs in France being vicious and full of rabies, so I stood stock still. Out of the house appeared a well-rounded woman with olive skin and jet black hair swept back into a bun like a Spanish dancer. 'Bayard!..Tais-toi!', she yelled and the dog was instantly transformed into a friendly teddy bear. This was Solange, the farmer's wife and life and soul of the farm.

After a few nervous formalities, she showed me to my room at the back of the house, overlooking a small courtyard and I quickly set about unpacking. An hour later, Marcel, the farmer and his son, Jean-Marie, returned from the fields and we all introduced ourselves. Finally, Alain, a trusted farm hand, appeared with a family cousin, Régine, who was staying for a few days - and the household was complete. We all sat around a large rectangular kitchen table eating a wholesome meal washed down with plenty of rough red wine and talking well into the night. I had thought that my French was pretty good, but I soon realised that they spoke very quickly and in a strong local dialect, peppered with colourful slang and southern argot. Over the following days, I began to slowly tune in to this chatter and, before long, I felt quite at home with my adopted family.

I began to relax into the rhythm of life and work on the farm, which revolved around the timeless tasks of feeding and milking animals and harvesting crops. On the face of it, it seemed slow and lazy but I realised that people in these warm southern climes were used to pacing themselves, working in the cool and resting in the heat. Typically, Marcel would be up at around 5 a.m., milking cows and feeding. At around 8 a.m., he would be sitting down, dipping large hunks of bread into a bowl of black coffee, before going out to work for another three or four hours. At lunchtime, he would return to the table for bread, cheese or maybe a salad and some fruit, washed down with red wine. Marcel only used conventional cutlery when really necessary, preferring instead to use his old Opinel pocket-knife for slicing his food.

I found it interesting that the bread we ate was never in the form of a baguette. In fact baguettes, because they don't keep for long, are mainly eaten by townsfolk. People living in the countryside who can't easily pop to the boulangerie every day, usually prefer larger round *pains de campagne* which last for several days if they are kept cool. Our farmhouse table featured a huge bread drawer and Solange would pull out a loaf the size of a car wheel which she sliced with a machete-like blade. After lunch, if the weather was hot, it was not unusual for everyone to disappear into the cool shuttered bedrooms for a lie-down and a doze, usually stirring again in the late afternoon. Then work would begin again and continue until the main evening meal at around 7 p.m.

Family life was focussed around the large kitchen table and, after dinner, we would chatter and laugh and play cards until late.

There was a small T.V. in the corner of the room but, apart from when we watched a couple of silly films, it was never switched on during my stay. I adapted easily to the life and became addicted to coffee. Nowadays I'm not a big coffee-drinker and can't stand the 'instant' granular stuff – but, on the farm, we drank our morning coffee in soup bowls and we dipped bread in it. The door was always open to visitors and it was not uncommon for the baker from Monbazens or a worker from a nearby farm or any number of relatives to be sitting down to eat with us.

I had made up my mind that I would eat and drink whatever I was given and, in general, I loved it. Most of the food was home-produced, including pork, turkey, and rabbit. In the courtyard below my bedroom were wire cages containing rabbits. When it was on the menu, Solange would open a cage, select the poor bunny and quickly dispatch it. There was an iron hook driven into the wall and the rabbit would be hooked on it, gutted, skinned and trimmed, all in a few seconds. I must say that the process was so quick and skilful that the animal would have known nothing. There were plenty of fresh eggs, seasonal fruit and vegetables and milk from the cows. Wine was kept in barrels in a cool *sous sol* or basement reached by wooden steps from the kitchen.

One day, Marcel decided that the hard earth floor of the main barn should be concreted, so preparations were made. We took a tractor and trailer down to a nearby stream and shovelled clean sand and gravel, loading it back to the farm over a couple of days. Cement had been ordered from a merchant in nearby Monbazens so Jean-Marie and I set off on the tractor and trailer to collect it one afternoon. As we drove down the quiet main street, a shout rang out from a bar-café and we stopped. A jolly-looking man, part of a small group of locals, beckoned us over and, before I knew it, I was being interrogated. Was I the English man from the farm? How old was I? How did Jean-Marie know me? ..and so on. It seemed that news travelled fast in these parts and we found ourselves joining in with the chatter over a drink.. and another drink..and another. It was all very pleasant and we threw ourselves into it with enthusiasm.

After an hour or two, we reluctantly dragged ourselves away and continued on our mission to collect the cement. The tractor and loaded trailer meandered erratically homewards and, when we arrived back at the farm, I worried that we might be in trouble. We had been gone for hours and had turned up as drunk as skunks. In fact, Marcel hardly noticed and the work on the barn floor was simply postponed until the following day.

Work on the farm was extremely varied and I enjoyed turning my hand to whatever was asked of me. There were leisurely tasks like fetching cows back from the fields for milking, gently coaxing them homewards down leafy tracks. I learned how to milk them by hand, although this was generally done by Marcel and Alain. One day Marcel sent me off to fetch the large black bull back from a field and he suggested I took a good stick with me and not to be afraid to give him a tap if necessary. When I arrived, I spotted the beast in the far corner of the field, staring fixedly over the fence at a few cows grazing in a neighbour's field. Clearly he had one thing on his mind and I was about to interrupt his train of thought.

I strode over to him and introduced myself. No response. I explained, as politely as I could, that he might wish to accompany me back to his nice straw-lined stall – please. No response. Realising that he probably didn't understand English, I said, 'Viens!' and gave him a tentative tap on the rump. No response. Far too interested in the gorgeous grazing gals next door. I yelled as loud as I could and gave him a hard smack with the stick. There was a pause and then his head slowly turned to give me a condescending gaze, showing the shiny copper ring in his nose. There was a very deep, dark 'Moooooooh'. He took one last lustful look at the cows and then, very slowly, turned his massive bulk towards me, hesitated - and walked past as though I didn't exist. He knew his way home and he made his way in his own sweet time.

I persuaded him to enter his wooden stall where he had to be secured by a chain around his neck. Edging into the stall alongside him, I explained that, even though we'd got off to a bad start, I really wanted to be his friend. As he began to noisily munch some feed, I managed to get my arm over his massive neck to secure the chain. With relief, I began to edge out of the stall but, as I came level with his belly, he purposefully leaned his entire one-ton weight sideways and began to crush me against the side of the stall. The heavy planks bulged and I really thought he would crack my ribs. Hardly able to breathe, I smacked and thumped him and at last he slowly shifted his body weight and I escaped. I believe to this day that he was sending me a message that *he*, the bull, was ultimately in charge. He had done what I asked but only because *he* chose to.

One day, one of the cows became very ill and we thought she was going to die. She could barely stand and was unable to digest or expel normally. Marcel had stuck a long needle into her stomach to get rid of any excess gas, but that didn't relieve the situation, so a vet was called. I had to hold the back end of the poor shaking creature by tweaking her tail, whilst the vet cut her open, layer by layer and removed large quantities of part-digested food. He was up to his armpits, scooping out the foul-smelling sludge. It seemed crude and brutal, but it did the trick and, once stitched up again, she soon made a complete recovery.

There came a time in July when it was necessary to de-flower the maize. I have no idea *why* it was necessary but all available hands were needed in the maize fields, plodding slowly down the planted rows. It was hard physical work in hot sun, wearing only a pair of shorts and a straw hat. The height of the crop meant reaching for the flowers and then pulling hard to remove them. This went on for days and, each day, we were all exhausted and ready for an early night after the evening meal.

We harvested the wheat using an ancient German machine towed by tractor. It should probably have been in a museum, was very slow and I was given the job of riding on one side of the wheezing contraption to bag up the grain as it was disgorged. The work was very hard and I was covered from head to foot in a film of creamy dust. It was only relieved by the frequent field-side stops to drink and eat from a hamper.

Hay production was far easier and I enjoyed driving a tractor fitted with a cutter. The hay had to be left for a while in the sun, then turned and eventually baled. Neighbouring farmers all seemed to share their equipment and help each other with no thought of payment. I remember once going with Jean-Marie and Alain to bring in the hay for an old man who lived and worked alone in a little tumbledown farm in a nearby valley.

When we had finished working, all the hay was safely in the hayloft above his house and we were invited in for a drink. It was a very simple room with whitewashed walls and the only furniture was a large scrubbed table in the middle of the room, six chairs and, surprisingly, a beautifully ornate and very expensive-looking antique long-case clock, ticking away in the corner. The only light was provided by a brass oil lamp hanging from the ceiling directly over the table. The old man brought plates of bread, ham and cheese and, of course, a jug of wine. As we set about the food and began to talk, a moth circled the oil lamp and began to irritate the man, so he rose slowly from his chair and shuffled off into the back kitchen. I was mystified when he returned bearing a shallow white bowl filled with water, which he then held out underneath the lamp. The moth promptly flew into the water and he shuffled off again out of the room. It's funny how some small moments stick in the memory.

Although I was living in a tiny rural community, there was no shortage of social interaction for a nineteen-year-old. During the summer months, most of the surrounding villages held fêtes in turn on Saturdays. They typically began with a fair and traditional music throughout the day. Then there followed a more raucous evening dance for the young ones, featuring a local band playing rock and pop late into the night. We would pile into Alain's wreck of a 2CV which had no lights, no reverse gear and a gaping rusty hole in the floor and set off to taste the action.

There were always girls to try to impress of course – friends of Régine and a scattering of female students who were back home for the summer from universities in Toulouse or Paris. Every Wednesday night our farm also hosted a dance with a live band. We erected a small stage at one end of the barn and Solange served up onion soup. There was plenty of beer and wine and we sometimes partied until 2 or 3 a.m. I remember meeting a pretty girl at one of these dances and, at breakfast the following morning, someone mentioned that they hadn't seen much of me in the barn. Marcel tapped the side of his nose knowingly and said, 'Il était dans la salade avec Marie-Christine'. Literally, 'He was in the lettuce patch with Marie-Christine'.

On Sundays, we often made excursions 'en famille' to visit relatives for long sociable lunches or we went swimming in a nearby mill pool or off to rivers to fish and swim. These were happy times and I was, by early August, feeling settled and contented with life. In those days we hardly used the telephone except in emergency but I had scribbled letters home to my family and friends. Before leaving the UK, I had arranged with Phil Parker that he would fly out to Marseille and we would continue to explore for another three weeks before driving back through France together via the farm. As the time of my departure grew closer, I began to dread leaving. Solange and the family had made me so welcome and they said that I should stay for longer.

I eventually left the farm on a mid-August Monday morning with the back seat of my little red car laden with provisions. Solange was like a mother hen and insisted that, to avoid starvation, I take three dozen eggs, fresh tomatoes, ten bottles of wine, milk, cheese, sausages, bread and a whole roast wild duck.

Thirteen

Singing for Supper

Making my way southwards I passed through delightful scenery ranging from deep gorges, forests, golden fields and then into scrub and maquis. The sadness of saying goodbye to the family was offset by the excitement of being on the move again. I entered the Camargue and began to look for a place to spend the night. I had heard stories of gypsies and bandits in this part of the world and it certainly had a wild and desolate feel about it. I had stopped about half a kilometre from a tiny walled village. The wind had increased to a whistle and there was even tumble-weed blowing around, so I decided to sleep in my car. I needed water so I walked into the village to fill my bottle from a pump in the middle of a cobbled square. There was no sign of life except for one face staring from an upstairs window but, as I was leaving, a shepherd drove his flock of sheep into the square and we exchanged a few words.

I walked back, sat on a large rock and feasted on cold wild duck, tomatoes and bread and drank wine to send me to sleep. I was wearing an old straw hat and a pair of patched jeans. It quickly grew dark and the wind was rocking the car so I locked myself inside and made myself as comfortable as possible. I kept my sheath-knife handy and drifted into a very fitful sleep.

The next day, after a quick swim in a nearby lagoon, I drove and collected Phil, complete with guitar, from the airport at Marseille. It was a happy reunion and we travelled eastwards over the next few days and then up into the foothills of the Alps beyond Grasse. We practised singing in harmony together, mainly Beatles songs and Phil played guitar as well as always, interspersing our songs with instrumentals like 'Sweet Georgia Brown' and 'Classical Gas'. We worked our way through Solange's provisions and stayed in a variety of small camp-sites.

In one of these sites, we were singing as usual and we slowly attracted a gaggle of very small children who were spellbound. Their parents were delighted that we were keeping them amused and, for a couple of days, we felt like teachers in a kindergarten. They sat cross-legged in a semi-circle around us, transfixed by the songs and asking us loads of questions. We were invited to parents' tents and caravans for meals and wine in return for a song or two. We had decided to meander back to St. Tropez and, on the way stopped at lovely little villages, like Aiglun and the small alpine town of Puget-Theniers, all the time fuelled by playing and singing for pure pleasure.

We soon realised that, through our music, we were meeting people from all over Europe, young and old who were not only listening but also joining in and offering us food and drink. It was great fun. Our daily practice routine was beginning to show results and we decided that, once back in St. Tropez, we would try our luck on the quayside. After a few more days, we arrived and, just out of town, on the Ramatuelle road, there was a small patch of dusty ground on which there sat an abandoned wreck of a wooden boat. We pitched our tent next to it and made that our home for the next few days. It seems incredible now that it was possible to leave a tent and a few possessions somewhere with little or no risk of them being stolen, but that was the case.

Apart from the painters selling their artwork, one of the star attractions on the harbour front in St.Tropez in those days was a lively little character calling himself *Coin-Coin*. He was made-up as a clown and he rode a mono-cycle, juggling and performing all kinds of stunts. He rode up the gangways of expensive yachts and headed full-tilt at the dockside, jumping off at the last second, catching the bike in one hand and so on. He was very good and attracted large crowds and hats-full of francs. We were nervous about entering Coin-Coin's territory, so we hung around shiftily until he moved on and then we positioned ourselves on the quayside and began our routine. We started shakily, but soon gained confidence and began to enjoy ourselves. This must have shown because, steadily, a crowd gathered and the old straw hat began to attract their money.

The time came when we had to start our journey home and I had arranged to call back at the farm on our way so that Phil would be able to meet Solange and the family. We were greeted like long-lost sons and spent two days helping out with odd jobs and swapping stories over long, leisurely meals. The day before we left, we all sat together under the oak tree at the front of the farmhouse, listening to Phil's guitar and singing together in the sunshine.

Marcel had cleared out an outbuilding and was about to throw away a rusty old water hand-pump, so I offered to buy it. He refused to accept any payment so we dismantled it and loaded it carefully in the rear foot well of the car. It would be a present for my father and, lovingly restored to shiny perfection by him, it was eventually installed at Waddington to draw rainwater from an underground cistern.

This was my second sad departure from the farm and, as before, Solange showered us with gifts of sausages, bread, wine, pastis and eggs. We drove back northwards and spent the next night in our sleeping bags on the hard floor of a half-ruined brick-built pottery. It provided a good warm shelter and somewhere for us to sit, eat and make tea. As we settled we could hear that we were sharing the building with rats but they kept themselves to themselves and, being so tired, we had no problem sleeping. On the 7th of September we pushed on and caught the ferry from Boulogne. I dropped Phil off at his home and then arrived at Waddington late that night. Mum and Dad were still awake so we sat and talked until two in the morning about all my adventures. Then there was the sheer bliss of falling into my own comfortable bed.

Having lived a life of leisure for a few months, money was tight, so I knuckled down to working for my father for a few weeks to help keep my head above water during the coming college term. I drove vans and small trucks, delivering and collecting machinery and I helped with any painting or cleaning. Even so, money would be tight, especially as I intended to take my car back to Leicester with me for the coming year. I hated having to hitch-hike and catch buses to get about and besides, the car would allow me to offer lifts to girls, opening up all kinds of possibilities. My student grant gave me the princely sum of £63.13s.4d per term and my rent was £30. Anything more had to be earned. Some of my student friends worked part-time in pubs during term time, but I relied on working for my father during holidays and occasionally playing in the band.

Life at home in Waddington was changing. My sister was going out with a lively Italian, Gregorio – her future husband - and my dad had become a keen member of the local sailing club, based at flooded gravel pits in North Hykeham. Fred, now aged fourteen, was obsessed by all things mechanical and was restoring a tandem, a BSA motorcycle and was re-building a pre-war Morris 8. As usual, my mother was the constant throughout, always there and always doing her best for her family as she had from the very beginning. Even at age nineteen and even though I was only forty miles away, I would receive little parcels by post every so often containing a ten shilling note and a few treats, maybe chocolate bars and chewing gum, always with a letter sending news and telling me to look after myself. Of course I told her not to be so silly sending me stuff but, secretly, I loved the fact that she cared.

Soon I was back into the familiar routine of lectures and late nights, meeting up with friends and listening to music. Girls came and went. There were flings and crushes and life was cheap and sweet and easy, although I probably didn't appreciate the value of it at the time. I was dating a Welsh girl called Meriel and we were invited to join a group of about thirty other students on a pony-trekking trip to the Brecon Beacons in south Wales. It was late November, very cold and, as usual for that part of the world, there was plenty of wind, rain and a flurry or two of snow. We met the rest of the group at a little pub and spent the next couple of nights huddled in sleeping bags on the floor of a large mountain hut.

I felt sorry for the poor farmer who rented us the horses and acted as our guide. We were a motley crew generally having little or no riding ability. One lad wore a motorcycle crash helmet with goggles and a full-length fur coat. There were others trying to stay dry by wearing fertiliser bags with holes cut for arms. There were leather jackets and all manner of fancy dress including, in one case, a night-dress. It was very muddy and slippery underfoot and I had a pony called Steptoe, who was very clumsy for a mountain pony. I remember, at one point, finding myself lying sideways in the bottom of a ditch with a kicking horse by my side. Anyhow, we survived the weekend and a good time was had by all – except, I suspect, Mr. Mills, the farmer – and Steptoe.

In December, there was a 'work to rule' strike by electricity workers and so power cuts began to affect life in our student house. We didn't possess a T.V. set but we missed our music, we couldn't prepare for lectures in the dark and it was very cold. There were even reports of hospitals being forced to function on batteries and candles and the disruption was set to rumble on throughout the seventies. The trouble peaked during the miner's strike and the three-day week later introduced by Prime Minister Edward Heath.

When the college term ended I drove back home to Lincolnshire for a three-week Christmas break and welcome reunions with my old school friends, Nick, Phil and Kevin. It was a white Christmas in Waddington and, after clearing the tennis court of snow and playing a silly game or two, we had a traditional family Christmas Day lunch lasting late into the afternoon. Fred and I then took Simon for a walk round the village lanes to get some fresh air. There was nobody else out and about and the village was perfectly silent under a carpet of fresh snow.

Fourteen

Pretty Serious

One Friday night in January 1971 I drove from Waddington to Nottingham, about thirty miles away, to visit my old Sea Cadet friend, Nick Kennedy. His parents had moved there a few years before and I had always kept in touch. In the evening, we went into the city and found ourselves in a very crowded 15th century pub, The Flying Horse (now a shopping arcade) in The Old Market Square. Nottingham had a reputation for its pretty girls, the theory being that the lace-making and textile industry, for which it had been famous, attracted female workers from far and wide. It was there that I met Anna and there that my connection with the city began. She worked for the owner of the local newspaper, *The Evening Post* and we began to see each other as often as possible.

On the 21st June, I sat my final exam and packed all my belongings to leave Leicester for good. I had been spending far too much time in Nottingham, sometimes arriving back in Leicester at 4 a.m. and then nodding my way through my first lecture which started at 9 a.m. Somehow, I managed to pass all the required subjects but still had no firm idea about what I wanted to do with the rest of my life. I applied for jobs and attended interviews but I really was finding it hard to focus on a future career.

In the meantime, I continued living at the family home in Waddington, doing odd jobs for the family firm. I enjoyed the work, driving a pick-up, delivering 45 gallon drums of fuel for Atlas diggers that were working out on the fens, or towing a mobile compressor back to the yard from a building site in Horncastle. Sometimes I had to help felling trees or removing hedgerows on remote farms. I received a letter from Phil Parker telling me that he was working in a nuclear power station in France.

At last, however, in late September, I decided to make a move, so I rented a small top-floor bed-sit in a large Victorian house in Magdala Road in Nottingham and began searching for work. On 2nd of October I bought a suit for the princely sum of £28 and, by the 11th of October, I was starting a new job at *Pretty Polly*, a large hosiery and lingerie manufacturer, based at Sutton-in-Ashfield, just north of Nottingham. The salary was £1000 per year, my job title was *Assistant Sales Office Manager* and there were three of us working in one room under a manager, Mr. Prentice. I soon realised that the work was fairly tedious in that we simply acted as administrators for the travelling sales force. The only perk for me was, every now and then, a new product would be launched and an attractive female model would be sent to our office to show it to us. I remember with a little embarrassment, being talked through the finer points of gussets and trims whilst nubile young girls were posing provocatively in front of our three desks, wearing nothing but balconette bras and lacy panties – but, hey – it was my job – and I was twenty years old.

Pretty Polly was then owned by Walton's Hosiery and the factory was huge. I was impressed by the banks of knitting machines, each capable of knitting about five miles of very fine nylon or polyester yarn into a pair of tights in less than one minute. Then there were hundreds of female machinists sewing for all they were worth to finish the products. There were still factories like this all over the Midlands in the sixties and seventies, all specialising in certain types of textile products. Sadly, the industry has all but disappeared from the area. Some of the older mills have been converted into fancy apartments and some have been demolished and confined to history. The Sutton-in-Ashfield plant closed in 2005.

I lasted just over a year in my first full-time job and, after working one month's notice, I walked out for the last time on 28th April 1972 with no better idea of where I was heading than on the day I had started. It's not that I was at all work-shy but I found it dull and was clearly not cut out for full-time office work. If nothing else, I had learned what I did *not* want to do and was now right back to square one. Anna and I were spending as much time together as possible and we even talked of getting married. She loved her job at *The Evening Post* and she was also a poster girl for the city, doing promotional work for the annual Nottingham Festival, even travelling to America as Maid Marion to do a T.V. appearance with the Sheriff of Nottingham. She was also a pin-up for the Royal Horse Artillery, at that time based in Germany, increasingly living in a world of champagne receptions and then dropping round to my third-floor garret from where we went out to pubs and cinemas.

I had to find a career and so, while I considered my options, I began a short-term job at Players cigarette factory in the city. I worked in the 'Slitter Department' in the bowels of the huge Victorian factory. This was where reject or faulty cigarettes were put through a machine to be separated into their components of paper, filters and tobacco ready to be re-cycled and re-manufactured into new, first quality cigarettes. It wasn't the most glamorous or rewarding work on the planet and I seemed to spend most of my time cleaning machinery and sweeping up. It was extremely hot, the air was thick with tobacco dust and we were given no protection except a pint of fresh milk to drink each day to help settle the dust in our dry throats. I was also allowed to buy two hundred cigarettes a week at a very low price. I was not a smoker but I took them anyway for Anna's parents who both puffed away like chimneys.

I have no idea when I first ate in a restaurant, but I do have vague memories of trying to impress Anna in the 1970s by treating her to a 'Berni Inn' type meal where the choice was very limited by today's standards. The height of extravagance would be Prawn Cocktail to start, followed by Rump Steak and chips and a dessert of Black Forest Gateau. Wine was rarely drunk and, when it was, the chances are it would be Blue Nun or Mateus Rosé. Popular drinks in clubs and bars were lager and lime, rum and blackcurrant, gin and orange and Bacardi & Coke. A few of the more adventurous pubs began serving tempting meals like scampi in a basket in addition to the usual packets of crisps. Life was good and, with more immigrants coming into the country from India and Hong Kong, restaurants began to spring up in cities and towns selling tasty spicy dishes unlike anything we had tasted before. It's hard to believe that, through the late sixties and seventies, buying fresh foods like tomatoes or strawberries out of season was almost unknown. Supermarkets as we know them had only just begun to appear and, even there, choice was limited.

The job in the cigarette factory lasted until late July when I gave up my rented room and headed back to Lincolnshire for a few weeks work with the family firm again. Everything was changing. The UK had, at long last, been taken into the European Community in January by Edward Heath after being twice rebuffed by General de Gaulle of France in 1963 and 1967. Our currency had been decimalised in 1971 and there had been widespread industrial action by car workers, coal miners and post office worker amongst others. There were sporadic bomb-attacks by the I.R.A. as the troubles in Northern Ireland continued to simmer after the 'Bloody Sunday' killings in Londonderry.

In the midst of this turbulent period Anna and I were heading in completely different directions. She was on a high and I was going nowhere fast – so, after a couple of years together, we parted.

On a happier note, my sister, Susan was married to Greg in January 1972 and so, at a stroke, our family had inherited a host of Italian in-laws and friends. The couple set up home together and she threw herself into learning the language and cooking pasta dishes for one and all.

In September, I began working as a trainee surveyor for a fledgling civil engineering company, C.I.S., later known as Linpave, based in Scampton village, just north of Lincoln. In stark contrast to the gruelling admission procedure for the Royal Navy, the interview had simply consisted of a fireside chat at the home of the owner, Tony Beetham and, from the start, it felt right. I had an H.N.D. in Business Studies but no civil engineering qualifications so we agreed that I would begin by doing physical work with the two or three gangs he employed whilst working towards a qualification.

I signed on for a six-year, day-release course to qualify for the Institute of Quantity Surveyors at Nottingham Trent Polytechnic. From the very beginning, I loved the work and I threw myself into it enthusiastically. My time was divided between acting as an assistant surveyor to the boss, travelling with him to the various sites, hard physical work with a drain-laying gang or a surfacing team, some office work, helping to estimate for future projects and then, every Wednesday, driving off to Nottingham for QIS studies. The variety and the fact that there was plenty of time spent outdoors suited me perfectly. Tony was always approachable, the business was attracting plenty of work and thus I was encouraged to learn quickly and take on responsibilities as soon as possible. My starting salary was £1200 per year.

With a steady job and, once more enjoying my mum's home cooking, life was pretty good. My brother, Fred had started a course at Lincoln Technical College and was still spending all his spare time tinkering with all things mechanical. He had a circle of close friends with odd names like 'Maggot' and 'Wood-Gnome' and they all sped around on battered motorcycles and mopeds. I started dating Chris, a sixteen-year-old girl from Waddington village. She worked in a florist's shop in Lincoln but became allergic to flowers and so trained as a nurse. Conveniently, I was able to reach her house by hopping over the low stone wall opposite our house and crossing a small paddock and, although she was six years younger than me, we hit it off immediately. Her parents made me very welcome too and my hops over the wall became more and more frequent.

Around this time, I worked my way through a selection of second-hand cars – a Ford Anglia Estate, a Morris Minor Traveller, a VW Beetle, a Mini Van which blew up in Newark and a lovely old Rover 60, bought for £60. It had a beautiful wood and leather interior, a freewheeling drive system and a large rust-hole in the floor to let the mud in. It also had the disarming habit of allowing the rear nearside passenger door to fly open on sharp bends and it drank fuel like a Sherman tank.

I'd had my eye on a lovely 1957 MGA sports car and, mustering my finances, I went for it. I think I paid £400. It was in really excellent condition and was finished in a very eye-catching 'Surf Blue', a sort of turquoise aimed at the Californian market. I loved it and, even in colder weather would whizz around with the hood down, wearing a woolly hat to keep my

121

ears warm. One summer, a couple of years later, I drove the MG on a two-week camping holiday to the south of France again with Nick Kennedy.

Work went well and I also looked forward to my Wednesday visits to college in Nottingham. It broke up the working week, lectures began at 9 a.m. and ended at 8 p.m. and so, with the travelling, it was a long day. I became friendly with a fellow student, Graham, who looked like a young Robert Redford and had a laid back manner and a ready wit. He was also adept at doodling and drawing caricatures of all the lecturers. Naturally, when lectures finished, we went out on the town together and I soon began to meet a new circle of friends and continue my close connection with the city.

Linpave was a success, expanded quickly and, by 1974, we were working on projects all over the East Midlands and further afield. I was taking on more responsibility as my experience grew. I was summoned to Tony's office and he presented me with a simple choice. He was confident that I was ready to take on much more and wanted me to become a Contracts Manager. If I decided to continue with the IQS course, that would be fine because I had only completed Part One, the first two years. However he would be happy for me to call it a day at college and continue learning on the job in return for a substantial increase in salary, a share of profits and a company car.

I didn't hesitate and decided, there and then, that my academic life was over and I would focus on work and business. Before I knew it I was driving a green Ford Cortina GXL company car and I was managing contracts right through from pricing and tendering for new work to final completion. It was very satisfying because it involved so many different disciplines: estimating, surveying, sourcing materials, meeting clients, inspectors and utility providers – and so on. There was a creative satisfaction in completing a given project on time, whether it was an estate road, a county picnic site, a sewage scheme or a new tennis court – seeing the final result and, hopefully, making a profit. As with any job, there were pressures and problems and timetables and budgets, but there were lighter moments and memorable incidents too. I had won a contract to re-surface a school playground in Boston and had a small tarmac gang on site. Usually the work would have been done during summer holidays, but this time we were asked to do it urgently in term time – which meant we had an audience. Preparation for the re-surfacing involved spraying the old surface with a very unpleasant black, sticky substance known as cold tar emulsion. This was sprayed on using a hand-pump fitted with a spray nozzle mounted, with a 45-gallon drum full of tar, on a trolley. The contraption needed three men to work it – one to pull the trolley, one to pump like hell and one to work the sprayer. It was a cold morning and the usual gaggle of curious pupils had gathered.

Billy began to pump for all he was worth and the pressure built up nicely - but no tar sprayed. As you can imagine, these machines were prone to blockages – usually cleared by whacking with a big hammer or, as a last resort, dismantling and pumping diesel fuel to try to clear the tubes. The reluctant pump was duly whacked and Billy kept on pumping in the hope that sheer pressure would do the trick. The whacking and pumping went on for a minute or two and then –BOOSH! Out from the burst pipe flew the black gunge covering all three men from head to toe as they tried to dance away. There were loud cheers from the enthusiastic young audience and choice expletives from the poor victims. I have no idea how they managed to clean themselves, but it wasn't unknown for these rough and ready characters to wash themselves down in diesel fuel.

I was soon given the job of managing all the ground-works on a new housing development of 250 houses in Lincoln. We had to clear and set out the whole site and then construct the roads, paths, fences, sewers and other services, everything up to floor level – then the builders took over. It was quite a responsibility involving different skills and lots of men and machines. There were truck-loads of bricks to receive and stack by hand and I employed one of my brother's ex school pals, 'Brock', for a week or two to help. He insisted in turning up to work wearing a top hat and tails, which caused some amusement. I had no complaints though because he worked hard and did everything asked of him. However, the tail suit and hat took a battering and ended up a grimy brick-red and very ragged, giving him the air of a gentleman tramp.

There was a little old Irishman called Martin O'Hanlon who was quietly-spoken and slower than the younger men, but was skilled at building and finishing man-holes and drains. He would sometimes go missing for hours and it was not unknown for me to scour the site and eventually find him happily fast asleep at the bottom of a man-hole. There were always problems of absenteeism, usually on Monday mornings or Fridays, after pay-day and I remember one incident which upset me. I had taken on a particular gang of self-employed ground-workers led by a real hard-case and part-time wrestler called Terry.

There was a dispute about quality of work and money and I had made a stand. I hated any arguments but sometimes firmness was needed and, even though I was still only in my early twenties, I was usually able to stand up to older men when necessary. Terry was indignant and stomped off the site to a local pub. I had made up my mind that, if he was late or drunk, I would have no choice but to fire him on the spot.

A few hours passed and then I spotted him lurching towards the site office. He burst in and loomed over me threatening me with a good pasting if I didn't agree to his terms. I was trapped and I decided that the best course of action was to remain seated, because I figured that even a drunkard might not attack someone who's sitting down. I tried not to let my fear show and, as calmly as possible, told him that I had no choice but to fire him - and I really thought I was doomed. He bawled and cussed and breathed beer-fumes and I'm certain that, if had stood and faced up to him, he would have beaten me senseless. In the event, he blustered, smacked the wall and lumbered from the office never to be seen again.

I had been looking around for a home of my own and, when I was 24, I found a lovely eighteenth century stone cottage in the beautiful small village of Burton-by-Lincoln, just north of Lincoln. There had been a settlement and a church there since at least 1068 A.D. when it was recorded in The Domesday Book. The house was the end one of a small terrace built on a hillside and facing south, not far from the ancient church. Originally a farm-worker's cottage, it was just a shell but the structure was sound, the walls were two-feet thick and it sat under a traditional pan-tile roof. The location was perfect for me and I managed to clinch the deal at £9,700. I relished the thought of working hard to make it my own and I couldn't wait to show it to my parents. I remember standing in the front garden with my dad and he just slowly shook his head and said, 'Rather you than me, lad'. I was so disappointed that I made up my mind there and then to prove him wrong. He had never been afraid of hard work and neither was I, so I set about transforming it and, before long, I was happily living there in comfort.

One winter, I was stranded in the house for three days with my car buried under snow on the new driveway. The village was completely cut off under a thick blanket of snow and there was no way of leaving to go to work. The cottage was warm, I had a lovely open fire and a good supply of logs. Even so, after a couple of days, I began to feel restless and, one afternoon, after donning a thick ski jacket, warm hat, gloves and boots, I set off to walk into Lincoln.

I soon realised why the village was inaccessible. The snow was almost waist-high and the old red telephone box at the top of the hill had completely disappeared under a drift. I waded onwards but the couple of miles to the *Duke William* pub which would only have taken me five minutes by car, took hours and hours. The *Duke William*, on Bailgate at the top end of Lincoln, had become a favourite meeting place for me and, having been sent a little stir-crazy, I was determined to sit down over a pint or two with friends. The snow had drifted across the road to the top of the stone walls at each side but I eventually made it and staggered, drenched from head to foot, into the bar. Fuelled by a few drinks and warmed by friendly conversation, I then had to face the silent, daunting trudge home in the dark, but the beer had gone down well and it had been worth it. Coincidentally, my brother, Fred, was getting serious with a girl called Susan, who was born and raised in Burton. And so, in 1983, they were married in the old village church opposite my house.

Sue had a sister, Margot, who worked for a local veterinary practice and I heard through the grapevine that she was trying to find a good home for a newly-born kitten. It seemed that a litter had been found abandoned and they had all been disposed of in one way or another. Margot was about to burn the box that had contained them, when she noticed something in a fold at the bottom of the cardboard. One tiny creature had gone un-noticed. It was the only pure black kitten in the litter and she decided that he deserved to be cared for. I volunteered and so began my partnership with Ted. I say partnership because I don't believe anybody could ever *own* him.

126

When he first arrived he was no larger than a tennis ball, sitting in my hand, but I nurtured him and he grew and grew until he became a small panther – sleek and lithe and majestic. He was a farm cat through and through and spent most of his time outdoors, prowling and pouncing. He soon became more or less a 'one man cat' in that, I guess because I fed him, he tolerated me and I knew how to handle him. He would happily let me stroke him and pick him up. We understood and respected each other but woe-betide if anyone else tried to go anywhere near him. He would growl and bite and scratch.

The only other person who stood a chance with Ted was my next door neighbour in Burton, a widow called Jenny who lived with her young daughter. Jenny was a great neighbour and, whenever I went away, she would make sure that the cat was fed and watered. I once returned after a few days away and I asked her if Ted had behaved himself. Unfortunately, he had not. Jenny had been visited by one of her aunts. Ted had seen his chance and lay in wait behind a blackcurrant bush alongside the path to the front door. As soon as the aunt came abreast of him, out he pounced, sinking his fangs into her leg and clinging on like grim death. The more she squealed and kicked, the more he hung on and Jenny had to resort to a broom-stick to dislodge him.

Even Ted, although big and strong and independent, had his vulnerable side. One very stormy night I was safely tucked up in my bed whilst the driving rain and gale-force wind wrought havoc outside my window. At around 3 a.m., I thought I heard a cat howling. I went to the window and strained to hear anything above the roar of the storm and then I just detected the faint but pitiful howl. I threw on something warm, went downstairs and out into the back yard. Ted was stuck up one of my neighbour's overhanging trees and was pitifully crying his eyes out.

I went and fetched a ladder from the garage and wobbled up to retrieve the poor stricken creature. Now the thing about cats is – they're stupid. Their claws are curved and are very good for climbing *upwards*. Getting down is a very different story because, what they should do is go down in reverse, using their claws in the same way to hang on, but, what do they do? They turn round and try to descend facing forwards. No grip whatsoever – so either they plummet to earth or they freeze and just yell for help. That's not where it ends however because, when help arrives, they attack it – so I'm at the top of a swaying ladder overhanging my neighbour's garden at 3 a.m. fighting with an angry panther in a raging tempest. He hissed and bit and scratched. It took a while…

In the late seventies, it became apparent that things were not going quite so well for my father and his business. The winter of 1979 became known as the 'Winter of Discontent', so dubbed after the opening lines of Shakespeare's *Richard III*, 'Now is the winter of our discontent.' There had been widespread public sector strikes and the economy had suffered very badly during the period from 1974 to 1979 under the Labour governments of Harold Wilson and James Callaghan. In May, the Conservative Margaret Thatcher came to power and, for the next ten years, set about tackling inflation and privatising state industries. Unemployment soared and with that came a severe recession and economic hardship.

Blades and Waite, like many small business up and down the land, suffered a dramatic decrease in income whilst high inflation meant that costs were increasing relentlessly. The plant and workshop manager decided to leave and a few drivers were made redundant. Dad took all this very badly. He began to disagree with his partner and his health began to suffer. In retrospect, it was a bad decision, but my brother, Fred and I decided to begin working for the family business to try to rescue the situation. We worked our notice, walked away from our secure jobs and made the move. It was a big gamble and it was agreed that we would focus more on contracting and developing industrial units to let out and less on plant hire, which had become hugely competitive. Fred had qualified as a surveyor and had been working for a large civil engineering company, A. Monk & Co., so, with my experience of estimating and contracting, we felt quite confident that we would be able to make a difference. We worked our socks off and succeeded in winning contracts – but prices were being squeezed so hard that it became more and more difficult to turn a profit. In short, we were fighting a losing battle. Our employees were earning far more than we were and, after two or three years, we reluctantly put company into voluntary receivership, Dad and Ray retired and Fred and I had to think again.

Fourteen

Crazy Diamonds

Although I was no longer spending each Wednesday at college in Nottingham, I still had plenty of friends there and enjoyed visiting the city. It was decided that we should keep the mid-week tradition going and so began the routine of meeting up for a meal and a few drinks each Wednesday evening. Now and again, we would meet at the halfway point of Newark, but usually I would drive over to Nottingham. It was a seventy-odd mile round trip just for an evening out but it was worth it. The breathalyser had been introduced to the U.K. in 1967 so the police were not so free to use their own discretion about driving under the influence of alcohol as they had been through the fifties and early sixties. For years, in rural Lincolnshire, social life had centred round long evenings drinking in distant pubs and then driving the many miles home. Occasionally we would hear stories of people driving into trees and hedges but, in general, there were few serious incidents.

With the stricter rules in force, it seemed sensible to stay in Nottingham after a night out and then drive back to work very early the following morning. Through Graham at college, I had met a mixed bunch of characters, some of whom would turn out to be lifelong friends. One of these was James (Jim) Hazelden,

an affable and gregarious soul who bore a striking resemblance
to the young Phil Silvers or Sergeant Bilko. We called him Jimbo
or, much to his irritation, 'Bilko'. He worked as a sales rep for
a textile company, selling fabrics all over the Midlands and he
invited me to crash out in his spare room whenever I needed a
bed for the night.

By that time I had no serious girlfriend and there followed a
long period of brief encounters and one-night stands. I was still
unsettled even though I was in a steady and satisfying job and I
had a comfortable little house, but I seemed reluctant to commit
to a long-term relationship. Between Lincoln and Nottingham
I threw myself into having a good time, 'pubbing, clubbing
and partying' with gusto and I met quite a few girls who were
likewise hell-bent on fun and games.

The Nottingham club scene was varied and vibrant so we
spent our time between *The Hippo*, later known as *Mr. Millers*,
Babel, Arriba, Madison's, The Monastery and others. But my
favourite was a quirky little place called *Food for Thought* down a
narrow back alley, Hurts Yard. We got to know the regulars there
and, apart from the usual music and dancing, you could play
board games and, if you stayed late –or rather, early- enough
you would be served with a full cooked breakfast. There were
other haunts like *Forman's Wine Bar* which was absolutely tiny,
with standing room only for about twenty customers.

Yates's Wine Lodge was another favourite, situated in a
lovely old building in Long Row. In the sixties and seventies it
was heaving with a cross-section of society, young and old, rich
and poor. It featured a downstairs bar area where, apart from
the usual ales and spirits, they served very cheap 'Australian
Sherry' from large barrels. Upstairs was a gallery with a cast-
iron balustrade overlooking the bar below and there played a
1930s-style trio of piano, violin and cello. The ageing musicians
were formally dressed in evening suits and bravely tried to bring

a little decorum to the proceedings by playing jaunty renderings of *The Teddy Bear's Picnic* and *The Sun Has Got His Hat On* surrounded by potted palms and aspidistras. Occasionally a pint pot of beer would be dropped from the gallery onto the throng below. Paradoxically, the building itself had once been the meeting place for the Temperance Society and had also housed a roller-skating rink.

One member of our group was Gordon, known as 'Smoker', a skilled tailor who had learned his craft in Savile Row, London. He worked with a partner, Doug, who was also a terrific tailor, but an incorrigible drinker. They shared a small garret of a workshop in the Lace Market district of Nottingham and it was not unknown for Gordon to turn up early for work to find Doug asleep under the cutting table, having crashed out there following a long night on the tiles. He would brush himself down, have a cup of tea and start the day's work, apparently no worse for wear.

Three of us once decided to go off for a few days camping in North Devon. Tony Smith was to drive us there in his Cortina Estate and Gordon would provide the tent. We duly arrived at a campsite near Woolacombe and began to unpack. Gordon's tent was a frame tent. The frame was fine and the canvas was sound, but it appeared that they were un-related. The fabric sat in huge folds on a frame that was far too small, but we made the best of it and went off to the pub. When we returned the rain started. Gordon had a camp bed, but Smithy and I were lying in our sleeping bags directly on the groundsheet. The rain became much much heavier and the wind intensified. The fabric flapped and the frame creaked and Smithy and I soon realised that we were sleeping in a river. There was a steady flow straight through the tent and we were completely soaked.

Clearly, not only had we had chosen the Devon monsoon season for our break, but we had pitched our tent in the middle of some kind of flood relief scheme. We huddled and trembled our way through most of the night and then, abandoning the tent, squelched our way into the car. At daybreak it refused to start and the foot-wells were full of water. Fortunately, we were on a slope so we managed to push and bump-start it out of the campsite and down to the village. There, we gratefully booked into a hotel, had breakfast and as far as I know, the remains of Gordon's tent are still in the field where we left it.

As time had gone by, my situation in Lincolnshire had changed to the point where I no longer had a job with the family firm and had sold my cottage in Burton – so I badly needed a new start. I bought a couple of tiny terrace houses in Gainsborough and renovated them to turn a profit. That kept me going for a short while, but my heart wasn't really in it. However, one of my Nottingham friends was Tony Pearce, an ever-cheerful man, originally from Devon, who spoke with a soft West-Country burr. He made his living buying and selling yarn and textiles. Tony had been living in a bachelor pad in the centre of the city and, when I hadn't stayed at Bilko's house, I had often crashed out at Tony's. He had even given me a key so that I would be able to come and go as I pleased. Tony worked with a partner, Guy, and together, they had built a very successful textile business which brought them a degree of wealth and a high quality of life.

At one of his many parties, Tony had met Sue and, after a while, they had decided to get married – which caused a split with Guy and the business. The result was that Tony had begun trading alone and, yet again, he was doing rather well. So well, in fact, that he couldn't keep up with demand and he needed help. He suggested that I should join him, initially for a nominal wage whilst learning the ropes and then, after a year, as a partner. It was a challenge.

I moved to Nottingham, bought a run-down Victorian house in Devonshire Promenade overlooking a quiet park and threw myself into restoring it. For a year or more I worked hard with Tony, collecting and delivering heavy boxes of yarn and learning as I went along. It was hard physical work and I threw myself into it with a will but I soon realised that it was growing into a family business and I was, inevitably, destined to be an outsider. I sat down with Tony and explained that it would never really work. As well as a wife, he had a step-son and the business would naturally become a family firm so, yet again, I would have to find my own way forward.

The obvious solution was to start my own textile business. I knew the potential and I thought I had learned enough to make a start so I threw myself into it with enthusiasm. So as not to compete directly with Tony, I decided to buy and sell finished fabric rather than yarn and I set about contacting fabric manufacturers and buying up clearance lots to sell on to garment manufacturers, fabric retailers and market traders. Initially, I had no office or storage warehouse, so I worked from my new home and simply stored my pathetically small stock in the front room, which was still bare and un-restored, whilst I lived in a couple of rooms upstairs.

I worked hard but there was no let-up in my social life and I was meeting new friends all the time. Gordon the tailor introduced me to a whole gaggle of characters from his schooldays, including John Glover and John Stobart. We used to meet up in a pub called *The Hand and Heart* on Derby Road and there we made friends with some of the regulars. In those days 'The Hand' was presided over by a slightly eccentric Jim Fisher, who bore some resemblance to the lugubrious Clement Freud. The rear part of the pub is a cave excavated into the Nottingham sandstone and Jim had the bright idea of digging further into the rock to extend the pub. There would be Sunday afternoon 'lock-ins' where we would find ourselves drilling the back wall of the cave with a jack-hammer in return for free pints. When, years later, the Channel Tunnel was under construction, the newspapers featured a photograph of French and English engineers shaking hands through the opening as they joined up from either side. Jim commissioned a mural for the end of his 'Tunnel', showing two navvies with French and British flags, shaking hands through a trompe l'oeil hole in the rock. I guess it's still there now.

Things sometimes became very lively in *The Hand*, especially on Saturday lunchtimes whenever an international rugby match was being played. Jim would set up a T.V. and the place would be packed solid, deafeningly noisy and, if Scotland was playing, there would usually be a kilted Scot playing bagpipes. People do strange things under the influence of alcohol and Kieran Armstrong's obsession was 'bar-diving'. He would stand on the bar and just launch himself into the mass of humanity, trusting that he would be caught – which he usually was. I once saw Peter Gabriel do a 'stage dive' into the audience at a concert and I remember thinking at the time that it was a very courageous thing to do.

Always present at *The Hand* was Angus McKay, who, despite his Scottish name, claimed to be Welsh and was one of the funniest men I have ever met. He had a natural talent for telling stories and jokes and was a great mimic, injecting his tales with relevant accents and voices to great theatrical effect. Angus had the appearance of a bull-dog, with a large round head, seemingly no neck, a bristling handle-bar moustache and laughing eyes behind his glasses. He raced cars as a hobby, walked with a slight limp as a result of an accident in his youth and he had a French girlfriend, Estelle, who he always referred to as 'The Frog'.

He and his friends from Nottingham Rugby Club would often play elaborate pranks on each other, welding someone's metal gates together, ordering deliveries of farmyard manure to be dumped on a victim's driveway and so on. Their imagination seemed to know no limits, but the most extreme one I heard of was, to mark one of their mate's fortieth birthday, a group of rugby players overpowered the birthday boy and locked him in a large wooden crate. This they then delivered into the busy Old Market Square, in front of the City Hall and fixed a sign onto the crate proclaiming 'MARVO – THE ESCAPOLOGIST'. Of course, the poor guy inside had no idea where he was and, being ever so slightly miffed, yelled and cursed for all he was worth. Apparently he attracted quite a crowd. Personally, I wouldn't have wanted to be within striking distance when the box was opened.

One evening, an architect called Grogan arrived at the pub with red, angry-looking sores and scabs around his mouth. The poor chap could hardly speak but it emerged that he and his little gang had been for an Italian meal the previous evening and they had rounded off the meal with liqueurs. He had never heard of Sambuca before and so decided to opt for one of those. It arrived and the waiter duly set fire to the surface to heat up the floating coffee bean. Andy was fascinated and bemused. His pals assured him that it was normal to drink it whilst still flaming...

We had another friend, Mike Davison, known as Miriam and he turned up once wearing a brown paper bag over his head with eye-holes cut in it. I pulled the bag off to reveal a face, red and swollen, stitches across the top of the forehead and eyes black and virtually closed up with bruising. 'Miriam, what's happened to you? Was it a car crash? Have you been mugged? You look terrible!'

'No', he said sheepishly, 'I've had a hair transplant'.

After some weeks, unbeknown to us, Miriam's wife' told him she didn't like his new look and insisted that he have the process reversed as far as it was possible. Therefore, having spent a fortune once, he endured yet another procedure and turned up again, out of the blue, this time sporting a mummy-like head bandage painted with a big red cross.

In order to keep fit, I joined The Park Squash Club in Nottingham and I also continued playing tennis. Another friend, Bill, organised a small group to play golf on Sunday mornings. I can't say that the game itself captivated me, but I enjoyed being out on the course with good friends.

I had only played once before. One morning, I had received a phone call from Jimbo asking what I had planned for the weekend.

'Nothing much', I replied – 'Why?'

'Well, do you fancy a free trip to Jersey?'

'Yes, I've never been there. What's the catch?', I said.

'There isn't one – oh, except you'll be playing golf for England.'

'You *are* kidding!', I retorted. 'I don't know one end of a golf club from the other.'

At the time, Jimbo was working in the travel business and there was an annual tournament within the industry between England, Scotland, Wales and Northern Ireland. An England pair had suddenly been unable to play and Jimbo had bravely offered to step into the breach. He was as bereft as me when it came to golf, but at least he did own a ramshackle set of clubs. I was about to become the first international golfer in history who had never even laid hands on a putter. Now, I don't mind having a go at bluffing through a situation, but this was really stretching it. My new golf partner had reassured me that all we had to do was survive a couple of rounds and then we'd be treated to a free slap-up dinner. Everything had been laid on: flights, hotel, transport. Nothing to pay and nothing to worry about.

In fact, the less said about our performance at the Royal Jersey Golf Club, the better. Embarrassing doesn't even *begin* to cover it. I had to scrounge a set of clubs and we were constantly asking opponents for instruction as we went round. Jimbo was right that the free dinner was wonderful, but it culminated in a prize-giving ceremony. Needless to say, England came a miserable last and Jimbo and I were presented with a tennis racket apiece, with the implied suggestion that we shouldn't dare to darken the doors of the Royal Jersey ever again. Our international careers were over.

Fortunately, years later, the Sunday morning round of golf was much less demanding. We were gently coached along by Bill and none of us took the competition at all seriously. I remember one day, three of us were waiting for Jimbo to turn up. We were in danger of losing our tee slot, so we had no alternative but to start without him. We had played a couple of holes, when we spotted an unmistakable distant figure bounding towards us. It was Jim, but he was hobbling in a peculiar bandy-legged fashion, like a man with a hornet up his shorts.

He puffed his way to us and apologised profusely for being late. I asked him what the problem was and why he was walking strangely. The following exchange was probably the most surreal conversation I've ever had. He said,

'Oh, I've got golf tees in my shoes.'
'Why?'
'I was rushing and didn't have time to take them out.'
'Why are you late?'
'I've been to the hospital.'
'Oh dear, what's wrong? Nothing serious is it?'
'No, I had to take my mother'
'Well, what's wrong with her?'
'She broke her arm.'
'My goodness, how did she do that?'
'I ran over her.'

'What? You drove over your own mother? How?'
'I was in a hurry. She was saying goodbye on my driveway'
'Is she OK now?'
'Oh, yes, she's fine. Is it me to drive off?'

Sixteen

Planks

I was about twenty years old when I had my first taste of skiing. I had taken a course of lessons on an artificial slope in Nottingham with my girlfriend Anna and then we had flown off to Oberau, a small village in Austria for a week of falling on our backsides. I had broken my thumb on the artificial slope but, apart from that, I remember little of that first experience. A few years elapsed before I would be able to return to it but, once bitten by the bug, I looked forward to heading for the mountains almost every year.

So it came about that, a few years later, in the mid- seventies, my brother Fred and I booked a week in Söll, another pretty village in Austria. We shared a first floor room in a chalet that was home to a farming family and their cows. In the quiet of the night we were able to hear the contented beasts happily munching and doing all the other things that cows do, in the space immediately below our room. We were made very welcome and, each morning, after a hearty breakfast, we crunched through the sparkling snow a short distance to ski school.

The equipment we hired in those days was very basic compared to modern gear. The boots were just about ankle-high and made of leather. Nowadays, ski bindings are quite sophisticated and they allow you, in the event of a serious twist or fall, to pop off the skis to avoid a broken ankle or worse. Usually this means that the only resulting injury is to your dignity. Skis are nowadays also fitted with 'brakes' which, once the ski is released from the boot, dig into the snow to prevent the loose ski flying off down the mountain and slicing someone in half.

The earlier bindings only released the heel if you decided to perform a forward flip in a straight line ahead. Any other twisting manoeuvres whilst taking a tumble might easily result in permanent re-configuration of a leg or two. Furthermore, the skis then had no brakes and so, once let loose on the slopes without a pilot, they became dangerous missiles with extremely sharp edges. The only way to avoid this was to attach leashes clipped in a slack loop around the ankles. These were all well and good – but I have vivid memories of taking a fall to find myself tumbling and rolling down a mountainside with two six-foot long blades attached to my ankles and trying to protect myself as they clattered around my head.

One of our first ski instructors was a mature, red-faced character called Peter Mayer, a true man of the mountains who lived for skiing. He drilled his beginners thoroughly and, trying to teach the correct posture and balance, would be heard shouting in broken English, 'Bent zer kneez' or 'Arse to zer mountain – titz to zer town'. He always carried a hip flask filled with fortifying home-made schnapps and would often take a class of ten or twelve people back to his house for snacks and drinks. I remember sitting in his kitchen where there was a long high shelf lined with ski trophies. Most of them had been won by his daughter and he was clearly a very proud father.

Ski instructors, in general, have the patience of saints. Even teaching a group of beginners how to ride a chair lift is a challenge and I have seen novice skiers being dumped in writhing heaps at the top of the lifts. It only takes one of them to fall as he tries to dismount the chair and, unless the attendant quickly stops the lift, the following skiers just keep piling in. The first time our group was taken up on a chair lift to nursery slopes mid-way up the mountain it was a real adventure. We duly had our lessons and then, in the afternoon were given the choice of, either riding back down on the lift to the village, or skiing down a steep track complete with hairpin bends. Most of us opted to ski down and away we went – with the instruction to re-group at the bottom.

The track was quite icy, especially on the hairpins, so it was tricky but we all made it – except for Paul, an Englishman in his forties. We all waited and waited but he failed to show up. His friend said that he must have decided to take the lift down after all. We had been in the bar for more than an hour when he appeared looking hot and dishevelled. Apparently, he had lost control and shot straight off one of the hairpin bends, landing in the top of a pine tree, unscathed and still wearing his skis. Nobody else came by and it had taken him a good hour to drop the skis, slither down and make his way to the village.

Fred and I had watched some downhill racing on the T.V. now and again and we were intrigued by an Austrian called Franz Klammer. He didn't always win but he was just fantastic to watch because he gave the impression of being totally out of control. He had a style all of his own that might be described as 'random' and it always seemed to be a miracle that he completed a run without a major crash. There was also an Italian contemporary of Klammer called Herbert Plank – which has to be the best ever name for an Olympic skier.

Our skiing improved slowly and, in the following few years, more friends came along too, sometimes with wives and girlfriends, sometimes just a bunch of male friends. We enjoyed Söll immensely and went a few more times, staying at the wonderful 14th century Hotel Post. Today it has been totally refurbished, but then it was a traditional alpine inn with ancient stone arches and creaking painted woodwork everywhere. The place was very atmospheric and I remember a large circular table in the bar made of solid granite about 250 mm thick. With eight or ten people seated around it, it could just be shifted on its base. The après-ski scene in there was really lively and waitresses in traditional costume would rush around bearing half a dozen litres of foaming beer at a time in heavy-handled glasses.

The skiing just got better and better. As our confidence grew and we became more capable, Peter Mayer would take us to high remote snowfields and trails. There really is nothing more blissful than skiing very high up, under a warm sun in a perfectly blue sky. Pausing for a rest, there would be absolute silence – something that is increasingly hard to experience in this world. We would sometimes ski circular routes of twenty or thirty kilometres in those idyllic conditions. Peter knew the mountains so well and would lead us to remote mountain huts for a rest. I remember a group of us sitting outside one of these huts where a friend of Peter's lived with his wife. They brought out home-made schnapps for us to drink with our packed lunches and we looked down on a scattering of tiny dots of houses in the sparkling valley below.

Year by year I skied in different European resorts including Mayrhofen, Kitzbuhel and St. Anton in Austria, Wengen and Verbier in Switzerland and Sauze d'Oulx in Italy. During one of these jaunts in Mayrhofen, we were riding down from the very top of the mountain on the last cable car. We always made a point of ending our day's skiing at the very top station, having a few beers and then taking the dramatic ride down to the village. On one of these trips, we met a friendly gang of Dutch skiers who were collectively known as *Club Escolette* so, in retaliation, we formed our own, catchily named, *Ski Team Escargot* and, on future holidays, we had team stickers on our skis. Our logo featured a snail on skis heading bravely downhill at forty-five degrees.

In St. Anton there is a mid-mountain restaurant called *The Rodel-Alm,* which is a well-known watering hole for skiers. We went inside for something to eat by the roaring fire in the middle of the room and Bilko couldn't resist the roast knuckle of pork with all the trimmings. This brief lunch stop soon developed into quite a session. Beer and wine flowed freely and the whole place was buzzing, but the time came when we had to leave the warm fire and ski down to the village. The route down wasn't difficult, being mainly on a fairly gentle winding track. However, after a few hundred yards, there is a very steep drop off to the left which bottoms in a sharp gulley and then steeply up the other side to re-join the long loop of the downward trail.

I must emphasise that this is an *optional* route to be taken just for the hell of it. In fact it is known as *The Devil's Bottom* and it has no particular advantage other than it is steep, fast and exhilarating. We teetered on the edge, wondering whether to go and then a, one at a time, we went for it. You have to go for it to keep up enough momentum to shoot up the far slope onto the track and the G-force as you hit the bottom is quite something – especially with a belly full of beer and knuckle of pork.

One thing I will say about Bilko, he's always willing to have a go and, with a yell of, 'Geronimo!', he launched himself into the abyss. The downward part went quite well. He got into a nice tuck position for maximum speed and, even though his glasses steamed up, he held a true line. Things started to go pear-shaped when he suddenly hit the bottom, because he was thrown quite violently onto his back – so the steep ascent was made staring blankly at the sky. He hit the lip of the track just about ten yards in front of a family group making their sedate way down. So imagine if you will, the shock of seeing a large bespectacled person being thrown prostrate before you, seemingly out of nowhere - vomiting knuckle of pork. Fortunately he survived the experience and made his way, rather tentatively, down to the village. The poor young family on the trail, however, was probably traumatised for life.

Skiing, in common with other outdoor pursuits, is very weather-dependant and it is quite common to be bathed in hot sun in the morning under a clear blue alpine sky, only to find yourself struggling homeward through a 'white-out' blizzard at the end of the afternoon. The disorienting effect of a white-out can be very distressing and dangerous, requiring intense concentration even to remain upright, let alone make progress on skis. I have known it to be so bad that I have been barely able to see as far as my own two feet. It's no fun and I have always tried to avoid being caught out in such conditions but, occasionally, it just happens.

I was once taken with a ski group up high to ski the Hintertux Glacier in the Tirol which is open for skiing even in the summer. The highest lift reaches 3250 metres (10,660 ft) and, on the highest chairlift, which was very exposed, we were given quilts to throw over our knees. It was a strange experience because there was intense sunshine and a risk of burning the skin - and yet frost-bite was a danger. The air was fairly thin so any activity made me breathless, but the skiing was superb. Our instructor gave us free reign and I remember flying in huge arcs across the open snowfield flanked by great shining turquoise cliffs of ice.

Just as I was really enjoying myself, I thought I heard a shout and a whistle. Sure enough, the instructor was gesturing for me to stay closer and, just then, I whizzed past a crevasse – and then, slowing down, I saw another. It was a long crack a few metres wide and walled by solid ice in its dark blue depths. It appeared bottomless and, apparently, the glacial ice here is 120 metres thick in places, so I got the message and worked my way back to the safe area as quickly as possible.

Verbier, a picturesque resort in the Swiss Alps, is dominated by the imposing peak of Mont Fort which looms over the main ski areas. These are reached by a large cable car from the centre of the village. For a couple of days during one holiday, the village found itself covered by a very dense layer of low cloud and everyone huddled in bars and restaurants, seemingly unable to ski. We realised that the cable car was still open, so we kitted ourselves out and took the ride to the top. As we reached the snowfields, we emerged into bright sunshine and the cloud below looked like a white sea dotted with 'islands' formed by the lower peaks. Not only was it a magical scene, but it was totally silent and our little group of four or five friends had it entirely to ourselves. There had been a few inches of fresh snow overnight and it was untouched. All the lifts were working and the ski station restaurant was open – so we skied and skied, with fresh powder flying all around us. It was absolute perfection and we didn't meet another person on skis for the rest of the day.

We were not always so lucky with the weather and, in the French resort of Val d'Isère, a group of us had been caught out by a freezing blizzard. We were quite high up and we managed, after a long, cautious downhill run, to come across a welcome mountain hut which was warm and crowded with steaming skiers. One of our gang, Farmer David, was tapped on the shoulder by a Frenchman who gestured to his left ear. David had been wearing the obligatory woolly ski hat but his left ear-lobe had been left exposed. It was now adorned by a small icicle. The man told him to be very careful and not to try to snap off the icicle in case part of the lobe snapped off with it. The ear was warmed very slowly and carefully and there was no lasting damage.

That season was very cold indeed. We had borrowed my dad's big old Audi diesel estate car to drive there and, as we reached the closing stage of our journey into the French Alps, we realised that we needed to put anti-freeze in the fuel. We stopped at a garage to fill up and the lady on the pump suggested that an increased percentage of anti-freeze should be added because of the extreme cold they were expecting. We heeded her advice but, even so, that night the temperature sank to twenty below zero, the fuel froze and the car had to be collected by a local garage while we continued to enjoy our holiday. When diesel fuel freezes, it can't just be thawed out again. It forms a jelly that has to be flushed from the entire system, before fresh diesel is introduced.

I always like travelling overland in preference to flying. I suppose it goes right back to my early days of meandering through the French countryside and I think that the process of passing through landscape makes the journey and the arrival far more meaningful. We once took two cars, loaded with a total of six men, to the French village of Châtel, not far from the Swiss border. We arrived just before Christmas for a two week holiday, spending Christmas and New Year in a lovely private rented chalet overlooking the Vallée d'Abondance. When we arrived there was no snow and the weather was warm and sunny like a perfect English summer. For the first week we never saw a flake of snow and we had to amuse ourselves by hiking the mountains instead of skiing. In direct contrast, for the whole of the second week, the snow fell and fell. We had to dig ourselves out of the chalet and we had a high old time skiing in powder up to our waists.

On Christmas Eve, I managed to book us into a village inn where they laid on a special festive meal, so we were made welcome by the locals as they celebrated. It was a long evening and Stobart, one of our group, was notorious for sidling off early to bed where he would habitually snore like a hog. This particular evening, he refused the dessert and, saying his goodnights, headed off into the night. When we eventually arrived at the chalet, full of chatter and food and drink, we realised that Stobart was nowhere to be seen. We decided that he might have had a secret assignation with the waitress he'd been chatting to and we all retired. The next morning, Stobart appeared unscathed from his room ready for breakfast and we were keen to know how his evening had gone. It transpired that he had he staggered out of the inn, a little worse for wear and fully intending to make his way to the chalet. The street was crowded with people all heading in the same direction and, without realising, he had been carried along by the throng into the village church for Midnight Mass. There he had fallen soundly asleep, only to be shaken awake by a friendly parishioner on whose shoulder he had slumped for the duration of the service.

That wasn't the first time, or the last, that the dormouse in him caused amusement. Once, in Val d' Isère, we had been enjoying a similarly long evening meal when he announced that he was ready for his bed and, like Elvis, he duly left the building. The rest of us lingered on for another half hour or so to enjoy coffees and drinks and then we too headed into the night. We hadn't walked more than a few paces when we spotted Stobart, flat out and fast asleep in a deep roadside drift of snow. Having established that he wasn't dead, we half prodded and half carried him home to bed. I have many happy memories of holidays with Stobart and I remember skiing somewhere for a whole day, both of us dressed in formal dinner suits.

Naturally, the après-ski partying was as important to us as the skiing and there were plenty of encounters and liaisons over the years. However, before the fun began, it was sometimes a good idea to soothe any stiff muscles, bumps and bruises in a hot tub or sauna. In general, Europeans are relaxed about nakedness compared with the British. On one occasion in Mayrhofen, a few of us went to use the hotel sauna, which was presided over by a large, no-nonsense, Austrian frau. We stripped off and she ushered us into the steamy room where we found ourselves amongst a group of naked girls who had just finished work at a local shop. They were happily chatting and drinking beer. They offered us beer and we had a very sociable time, probably staying in the boiling heat for too long.

The girls eventually left and, after a few minutes, we finished our beers and went out too, only to have our way blocked by the big frau. 'Now zee must in ze snow go', she said. We had heard somewhere that it was common to go from the heat of the sauna into freezing snow - to stimulate the skin or something – and she was most insistent. She threw open a door, barking, 'Raus, raus!', and out we went.

'What a lark', we thought and began throwing snowballs at each other – before we realised that we were in a small public square. The sight of four very pink, very naked, men playing snowballs in the middle of their village must have been a shock for the locals. Or perhaps it wasn't.

Seventeen

Up

In 1976, my brother Fred and I decided to take to the skies. We had read stories of the early aviators and aces of the two world wars and we decided that we should have a go. Lincolnshire is littered with derelict and disused wartime airfields as well as those currently operated by the R.A.F. and so there is a rich history of flying in the area. We joined *Lincoln Aero Club* based at Sturgate Airfield, which was formerly R.A.F. Sturgate, a wartime bomber base, later home to the U.S. Air Force. About ten miles north of Lincoln, the club was small and informal and we were made very welcome.

Our initial training flights were in tail-wheel jalopies called Rollason Condors, designed in the 1950s and made of canvas and wood. They were fairly basic machines but nowhere near as basic as some others flown by club members. I remember one old boy had a tiny home-built aircraft powered by a VW Beetle engine. The tail-wheel was a castor from a drinks trolley and the top speed was not much faster than that of a moped. He was not supposed to fly it except in very calm wind conditions, simply because it would struggle to make any headway against a blow.

However, we heard that he had a party piece of executing vertical take-offs. Neither of us ever witnessed it but apparently, in a strong wind, he would prepare himself for take-off facing into the wind and, with the brake full on, take the engine up to full throttle. Then he would release the brake and pull back the control stick. Because the aircraft was so light, it just lifted off where it stood. That was all fine and dandy, but he would then find himself flying backwards or turning and racing off downwind with no chance of fighting his way home. It was a good story but I would imagine, if it happened at all, it was an accidental rather than a deliberate manoeuvre.

Over time, we graduated to Cessna 150 aircraft which were much easier to manage, chiefly because they sat on a tricycle undercarriage. This meant that they were on a level footing and the pilot could actually see where he was going during taxiing – always an advantage. At weekends we spent hours doing circuits, endlessly practising taking off and landing in all kinds of conditions. Then we were put through stalls and spins and how to recover from them. Looking at my old log book, a couple of lessons are marked 'EFATO', which stands for 'Engine Failure after Take-Off'. From what I remember, this was quite a tricky exercise whereby, after the usual take-off, when you were still climbing at full throttle, the instructor would suddenly cut the engine and calmly say, 'Engine failure'. Quick thinking is needed to stage a recovery. There is a natural instinct to try to make a frantic u-turn back to the airfield but, no, you must try to re-start the engine whilst selecting an emergency landing place ahead. I also seem to recall that 'carburettor icing' was a constant risk, meaning that fuel would be blocked off, stopping the engine and , every so often, you were expected to hold down a button to apply 'Carb Heat' to prevent it happening.

Soon, the day came when the instructor climbed out and said, in a matter-of-fact way, 'Okay, lad – It's all yours – do three circuits' He slammed the door shut and I realised that I was to fly solo. Trying desperately to remember all that I had learned, I was airborne before I knew it. The aircraft felt surprisingly light and a little skittish with only one person aboard, but all went well and I managed to land without incident. The next stage was flying solo cross-country, which involved navigating from A to B to C – a triangular course based on Sturgate. I remember having to land on a small grass airfield somewhere in Yorkshire, checking in with the controller there and then bouncing off down the grass strip to take off in front of an audience of strangers before whizzing back to Sturgate.

There was an awful lot to think about apart from just flying the plane. There were loads of safety procedures, radio calls to make, maintaining a good lookout, checking Ts and Ps (Temperatures and Pressures) and navigating using maps and visuals. It was all very rewarding but there was little time to relax and take in the view. We reached a point where we were both becoming strapped for cash. The hourly rates had increased a little and neither of us wanted to get into debt for the sake of a hobby so, reluctantly, we decided to call it a day. It had been a great experience and a real challenge but both Fred and I, years later, agreed that we had no strong desire to take up flying again.

Sailing, however, was another matter. Whilst Fred reverted to his first love of cars, motorcycles and all things mechanical, I always had a hankering for the sea. Dad was a member of a dinghy sailing club and, from time to time, I would crew for him. He had built a sleek and interesting boat called a Tempo Scow from plans and he loved racing it. It was like a large surf-board with a small cockpit and was a fast racer, but it was a wet ride and had a tendency to dive into a heavy swell, partly I think, because Dad had built it too heavy. It was his nature to over-engineer things 'just in case', so he had used solid planks of mahogany shaped to form the sides of the hull and so on.

The Tempo was a thing of beauty but, when racing, lightness is everything. Realising his mistake, he had sold it and switched to a Fireball. This was not so pretty but still had pace and was a more widely recognised class of boat. Later on, like me, he had become more interested in cruising and, a few years before, had seen a second-hand yacht up for auction at a machinery sale. It was a thirty-foot long Hurley, named *Jolie Fille*, built in the early seventies. She was in good condition but just needed a little T.L.C. so was an ideal project for Dad. He had placed the winning bid and transported her back to the quarry.

He had then started evening navigation classes and spent hours working into the night on the boat to bring it up to standard. It was at last launched at South Ferriby, in the estuary of the River Humber on the east coast. He soon sailed it down the coast to the River Orwell in Suffolk and based it at the marina in Woolverstone, with the idea of one day sailing to the warmer climes of the Mediterranean. *Jolie Fille* had a fairly shallow draught, having two small 'bilge keels' rather than a single deep central keel. This meant that she was well suited to shallow tidal waters and, when the tide went out, would sit nice and level on exposed ground.

It also meant that she was ideal for motoring through the shallower sections of the French canals. This would be preferable to risking the long voyage round to the Med via the notorious Bay of Biscay, exposed to the full force of the Atlantic and on through the Straits of Gibraltar. In any case, the French canal idea was vital if Dad was ever going to persuade my Mum to go along for the ride. This he duly managed to do and, in the early 1980s, off they went on their great adventure. They had a thoroughly good time, crossing the English Channel and entering the French inland waterway system at Le Havre. The mast had been dropped and secured on deck for passing under the main bridges and so the entire voyage was made under power.

Right into her old age, Mum used to reminisce about that first voyage in *Jolie Fille*, passing through huge lock systems in the canals and on the Seine right through the centre of Paris. They made their leisurely way on through the deep south, savouring the food and wine as they went down the Rhône and, eventually, out into the Mediterranean just west of Marseille. They found their way at last to the port of Altea, not far from Alicante, on the Spanish Costa Blanca. The boat was based there for quite a few years and they would fly off every so often to escape the cold of the British winter, or whenever they felt like a well-earned break. Spending time on *Jolie Fille* had certainly proved to be invaluable, especially for my father, when the business failed and later on into retirement.

In the late seventies or early eighties, my friend Stobart and I joined I.C.C. (The Island Cruising Club) based in Salcombe on the south Devon coast. Like me, Stobart loved sailing in all kinds of boats just for fun. We weren't competitive, so the relaxed atmosphere of I.C.C suited us perfectly. We would find ourselves there for long weekends and whenever we were able to spare the time.

The I.C.C. had been formed in 1951 by a small group of like-minded friends who simply wanted to sail and preserve classic boats. It was a great success and, by the time we came along, there were more than a thousand members served by an enthusiastic team of sailing instructors and volunteers. The boats varied from small single-seat Topper dinghies to racing keel-boats and two lovely classic yachts, *Hoshi* , an Edwardian schooner and *Provident,* a retired Brixham sailing trawler.

The club had an office, boatyard and clubhouse ashore, in Island Street but accommodation for members was in a former Mersey ferry, *Egremont*, which was permanently anchored in a part of the estuary known as 'The Bag'. People and supplies were shuttled to and from the town in a launch, *Shamrock* and dinghies were launched from a pontoon alongside the ship or moored at buoys nearby. Life on Egremont was fairly basic, with communal meals taken in a canteen where everyone had to take a turn at clearing up, washing dishes and so on. Sleeping accommodation was in small shared cabins each with two bunks and a small port-hole looking out onto the estuary. When we weren't sailing, eating or sleeping, we were usually drinking and socialising in *The Pugwash Bar* on board or in one of the pubs ashore.

Salcombe is one of the most picturesque towns on the south west coast of England. It lies close to the mouth of the beautiful Kingsbridge Estuary and, in the 1500s, was a simple fishing community which later expanded into a port, trading commodities with continental Europe. Between the two world wars it also began to develop as a holiday resort and sailing centre and, as with many coastal communities, the traditional fishing and trading activities have dwindled over time.

When I first began to visit, it would have been possible to buy a fisherman's cottage for less than £30,000 but nowadays, even ten times that figure would buy almost nothing. Properties with an estuary view are at an absolute premium with prices from a million pounds and much more. Whilst the place is still a delight, the 'gentrification' of the town has, in my opinion, severely damaged it's integrity and I feel so sorry for any young locals hoping to find work and buy their first marital home.

It's common for local residents in communities all over Devon and Cornwall to refer to tourists as 'Grockles' or 'Emmets' (Emmet is an archaic English word for ant). This poses a real question because the resentment caused by seeing wealthy outsiders turning up during summer months in their expensive cars is understandable. However, without these very visitors, there would be little or no work to be had anyway. Fishing is no longer able to support the community and tourism is therefore, a vital lifeline. There are efforts to address the housing issue and to diversify the local economy but the fact is that, despite being an area of outstanding natural beauty, the south west of England is relatively poor.

In the seventies and eighties, the sailing activities we enjoyed were sometimes unorthodox and would not be encouraged or even permitted today. My favourite was 'Pub Crawl Week' and, whenever we could make it, a gang of us would enrol. I recall that these 'courses' were run by a rather droll character, Beaumont, whose imagination ran wild when it came to devising novel activities and races. Apart from the three or four pubs in Salcombe, there were several others nearby, up the various creeks and inlets of the estuary. A typical challenge would be to race to the Millbrook Inn at the very end of South Pool Creek. It sounds simple enough, but we would be racing with no rudders. Rudders had to be un-shipped and left in the bottom of the boat. Any use of a rudder would be severely penalised by drinking 'forfeit' pints of mixed scrumpy – that strong, cloudy, head-ache-inducing, West Country cider – whether you liked it or not. Believe it or not, it is possible to steer any boat that has two sails, without using a rudder. It's a useful skill, but it takes practice and involves the clever use of the sails and shifting weight within the boat. On top of that, the estuary experiences strong tides and South Pool Creek partially dries out at low tide, so there is plenty of potential for running aground – again earning a forfeit.

There are several pristine sandy beaches in the area but there are also extensive banks of very gooey grey mud that are partially exposed as the tide ebbs. This mud is affectionately known by locals as 'The Putty' and getting stuck on the putty was never a pleasant business. Whilst most of Beaumont's forfeits were designed around alcohol, he had other weapons designed to humiliate and embarrass any 'losers'. After twenty minutes knee-deep in grey gunge, trying to re-float and bale out a capsized boat, Beaumont would chug along in a power boat and, with a devilish grin, instruct you to sail with your pants hoisted up the mast or do a headstand on the foredeck, as penance. A day's sailing during Pub Crawl Week always featured long lunch breaks in The Pugwash Bar or in one or two of the pubs around the estuary. There was also a competition for the crew that could sail to the most pubs in an allotted time, drinking a pint per person in each one and all without landing on the putty.

Each day began with a 'Briefing' and ended with a 'De-Brief'. Sometimes, my friend Stobart gave the briefing, standing, headmaster-like, in front of a large blackboard. He would chalk an outline of, say, Australia and add arrows for tornados, tsunamis, the jet-stream and other weather phenomena we were likely to encounter. Then he would mark the Race Course, which would naturally involve circumnavigating the entire continent. Hazards to look out for might include enemy gun-boats lurking behind headlands ready to attack and, if you were stupid enough to capsize, you would certainly be eaten by great white sharks. The 'De-Briefs' were no less frightening, in that they were, in fact, 'Punishment Parades' whereby Beaumont revelled in dishing out yet more madcap forfeits.

Our friend Mike 'Miriam' Davison was an occasional visitor too and he threw himself into all of the events with enthusiasm. Mike was very athletic, kept himself in good shape and was an excellent swimmer. We heard that the town staged an annual charity swimming race along the estuary, roughly from where Egremont was anchored to the town quay, a distance of maybe half a mile. It was quite a challenging event, well-organised with rescue boats on hand and competition was stiff – so we entered Miriam in the ladies race. We bought him a nice floral swimsuit and matching rubber hat and, when the big day arrived, we took him to the ship's galley and rubbed him all over with a thick layer of lard to protect him against the cold. If I'm honest, I think he enjoyed the attention a little too much, but anyway, the starting gun fired and around twenty women – and Miriam - set off like torpedoes. I was in one of the rescue launches and we cheered for all we were worth. He didn't disgrace himself but, sadly, he was beaten into third place by a couple of very athletic female sailing instructors from Egremont. He dragged himself out of the harbour to be towelled off and consoled by his team and then ushered off to the Fortescue Inn to recover.

One of Miriam's other talents was drinking a 'Yard of Ale'. For the uninitiated, this is a glass drinking 'trumpet' – about a yard long and resembling the old-fashioned post horn, but with a bulbous swelling at the bottom. Thought to originate in 17th century England, it typically holds about two-and-a-half pints of beer. The challenge is to drink the contents as quickly as possible without spilling any. The problem is that, you raise it and, just as you think the nectar is flowing nicely down your throat, it delivers a mighty rush all over your face, up your nose and all over your shirt. Miriam was one of a rare breed who was able to open his throat, like a sword-swallower, enough to take the volume in one go. In The Fortescue Inn, the long glass used to hang high behind the bar and there was, for some time, a notice alongside it saying, 'LADIES CHAMPION – MIRIAM - 12½ SECONDS'.

By way of a change, it was decided one fine evening, to take one of the club's large launches up the estuary to one of our drinking haunts, The Crabshell Inn at Kingsbridge. There were about a dozen of us in the boat, including the launch driver, Dan, who had a power boat permit. We had a high old time at the pub as usual and then Dan suggested we should be thinking of leaving because the tide was ebbing fast. 'Oh, don't worry', came the reply, 'We'll be alright for another pint'. He disappeared off to check the boat and a few minutes later, returned suggesting that we really *should* be leaving.

We trailed out of the pub full of contented wellbeing to see that he had started the engine and was casting off, desperate to leave. We all fell into the boat like so many sacks of potatoes and we were off. I suppose we made it for about five hundred yards and then a heavy lurch told us we were on the putty. Dan tried his very best to drive us off. We all moved forward to shift the weight, we moved to one side and then the other, all the time mumbling and giggling – still pub-happy and mellow. We were most definitely stuck fast and the tide was still going out.

Thankfully, the launch was well-equipped. He radioed to Egremont and reported our situation, he produced warm blankets to wrap around us and then there were wooden 'legs' to fit to the boat. Four of these were placed vertically to fit under the gunwale, or rim of the hull, to act as props. This meant that, as the tide receded, the boat would sit upright rather than flopping onto its side. During that night, we told every joke we knew and sang every song in the book. We listened to the water-fowl and studied the stars and watched the lights in the windows of Kingsbridge go out one-by-one. It grew very cold and seemed to last forever as we huddled together until finally, at around five in the morning we were once again afloat and able to motor back to Egremont. I have rarely been so happy to drink a cup of tea and fall into a bunk as I was that morning.

One day, Stobart and I were invited to help crew the classic Brixham sailing trawler *Provident* from Salcombe to Torquay for a classic boat show. We jumped at the chance. She was a traditional seventy-foot-long ketch, built in 1924 on the River Dart. She worked, fishing for the next few years out of Brixham, before being converted into a private pleasure yacht by a wealthy American. After the Second World War, Provident arrived in

Salcombe in 1951 as the founding vessel of the Island Cruising Club. In the 1980s, her skipper was a formidable young woman simply known as 'H', who made commanding this lovely old vessel look easy.

The voyage out of the Kingsbridge Estuary and round, past Dartmouth, to Torquay, went smoothly except, I recall, for one member of the crew. He was a young, gawky Australian with a tangle of fair hair and spectacles. We were sailing in slightly variable conditions and he was standing on deck, minding his own business, when the boom – the size of a telegraph pole – decided to swing. There was a thwack like a mallet hitting a melon as it struck his head and down he went. By rights it should have fractured his skull but in fact, he just stood up, shook his head and said, 'Well, I didn't expect that!'

Any sailor will tell you that you never stop learning and the day you think you know it all, you're in trouble. I remember that, sailing on Provident, I learned from H a new nautical term – 'Baggywrinkle'. It's a great word describing a useful object, namely a bundle of wool or strands of old yarn forming a soft protective cylindrical pad or cushion. These are attached to standing rigging wherever sails are likely to make contact, to help reduce chafe and damage to the sail. I always think it would make a lovely term of endearment: 'You old baggywrinkle ,you.'

When conditions weren't suitable for sailing, there was still plenty to do in the area. Of course, time might be spent having a full cooked breakfast in Captain Morgan's café, windows all steamed up, whilst thumbing through the newspapers just to pass the time. One day, I remember, when a gale was blowing and the rain was pouring, Stobart and I spent a whole afternoon playing bar skittles in the Shipwright's Inn with some locals. On such days, we would sometimes say, 'Well, there's nothing else for it, we'll just have to be village idiots', which meant we would spend the day ambling aimlessly and falling in and out of pubs and cafés. On days when there was no wind for sailing, we would sometimes take to rowing to town, or taking ferries and walking the beautiful coastal paths.

The coastal scenery is stunning and the wonderful South West Coastal Path passes right through Salcombe. This walking trail runs for 630 miles from Poole in Dorset, right round the south west peninsular of England, through Devon and Cornwall, to the Exmoor National Park back in the north of Dorset. I have an ambition to walk the entire length but, so far I have only had time to do a few short sections. I did spend a few happy days with my brother Fred one October, when we took four or five days off work to walk a section between Salcombe and Fowey.

I remember spending an enjoyable evening in The Blue Peter Inn in Polperro, an ancient fishing village with a notorious history of smuggling. We were made very welcome and I spent a while chatting to a local fisherman. He told me about the different catches to be had at different times of the year and I was surprised to discover that he couldn't swim. 'I'm amazed', I said, 'A fisherman all your life and you never learned to swim?'

With a knowing look, he replied, 'The idea's to stay *in* the boat, me'andsome'.

There were two musicians in The Blue Peter that evening, one playing acoustic guitar and another, a superb harmonica player. He wore a waistcoat with a dozen or so pockets containing his instruments. They ranged from a tiny mouth organ only an inch or so long, to a huge deep-sounding harmonica and he deftly whipped them out of the pockets as needed. It was one of those spontaneous occasions that really stick in the memory. Our few days of walking ended all too soon in Fowey, where we took the little ferry across the river, close to the cottage where the author Daphne du Maurier had lived. Then, after a last night in a comfortable B&B, we had to make our way back to Salcombe by bus and train before the long drive home to Lincolnshire.

Eighteen

Down

My little business was slowly expanding and, in the 1980s, I rented a basement near Sneinton Market in the centre of Nottingham. Known as 'The Banana Rooms', it had been used for storing and ripening bananas for the market and it was dark and dank – but it was secure and, more importantly, it was cheap. I had to carry all my stock up and down a flight of rough brick stairs but the exercise did me good and I was pleased not to be heaving the heavy rolls of fabric in and out of my living room. At last I was able to finish renovating my home and live in comfort. I had been transporting the rolls of fabric in my estate car, but soon I invested in a large van.

After a few years, space became tight at The Banana Rooms so I started looking for new business premises. Bigger space equals higher rent, but I happened to know a man called Simon Lane who was in a similar situation. He too was a sole trader and we had helped each other with various deals, so we agreed to share a warehouse. We found one that had enough height to take heavy duty racking and so, by splitting the rent and using the increased space and height, we were both able to store what we needed. It was a good arrangement because we trusted and helped each other without merging our businesses – something we were both reluctant to do.

I was working very hard, sometimes six or seven days a week and catching up with paperwork in the late evenings. I occasionally questioned whether I would have been better off working for a large corporation but, in my heart, I knew that I was more suited to working for myself. I was specialising in buying and selling clearance lines – fabrics that manufacturers had over-produced or that had been rejected for being an incorrect shade. I refused to buy second quality goods because it could lead to all kinds of problems and complaints from customers and so, slowly but surely, I built up a regular clientele. I made a concerted effort to spread my wings and it paid off. I even began to sell to a few customers abroad, notably in France, Belgium and Cyprus.

Even though I was pushing myself at work and renovating my house, I still found time to socialise and, one evening at a party, I met Lesley, who lived in Long Eaton, on the outskirts of Nottingham. She was attractive and intelligent and we immediately hit it off. Before very long, she sold her house and came to live with me at Devonshire Promenade. Lesley had a good job as a property manager for the Department of Employment so we both led very busy working lives and, like most couples of the age, in our spare time, we threw ourselves into winter dinner parties, summer balls and barbecues with friends. Life was treating us well, we loved each other and so, before long, we were engaged. Lesley was a wonderful person and it seemed that we were on course to spend the rest of our lives together. Even so, I began to have doubts. The old uncertainties began to haunt me and it didn't go un-noticed, so she became increasingly aware of my hesitation. It just wasn't meant to be. Lesley deserved a happy future and I just knew that I would end up letting her down – so we parted with heavy hearts.

I continued to throw myself into my work but it was a period of great sadness and uncertainty. It worried me that I seemed incapable of committing to a long-term relationship. Would I ever grow up? To cap it all, my father was becoming unwell. He was short of breath, had lost a lot of weight and began to struggle with even simple physical tasks. This was devastating for a man who had led a life moulded by hard physical work and outdoor exercise.

The previous year, he had moved his little yacht to Port Vendres in the south of France, not far from the Spanish border but he now hankered to sail it back to Altea in Spain, where he and Mum had made some good friends. He was planning to sail it solo and I became increasingly concerned that he would not be strong enough to survive, so I volunteered to go with him. A friend from Lincoln, Steve Finn was also keen to join us. Steve had no real sailing experience except that he had done a little wind-surfing, but he was fit and keen to have a go.

My father wanted the boat back in Spain before winter, so we arrived in Port Vendres one day in late autumn. I remember being shocked at just how badly my dad was coping. He was completely devoid of energy and had to stop to catch his breath, even after climbing a short flight of stairs. He was putting on a brave face, I could feel his frustration and it made my heart bleed. We provisioned the boat, checked the forecast and set off. Winds of force six were forecast for the following day but the boat was sound, we were well provisioned and we had no concerns. Out of Port Vendres, we steered south and then set a course past Barcelona, through an area known as the Balearic Sea which separates the Balearic Islands from the Spanish mainland.

The first day was easy and we all settled well into the routine. I remember that, for a good four or five hours, we passed through a huge mass of migrating fish. I have never seen fish in such numbers. They were all around us as far as the eye could see, leaping and diving, heading in the same direction, hour upon hour. If we had had a fishing net, we would have been able to catch literally tons of them. I believe they were albacore tuna, very fast and sleek, each generally between two and four feet long. It was a truly amazing spectacle of nature.

That night, the wind increased significantly, gusting up to a force-8 gale. By the second and third day we were continually fighting very steep waves up to four or five metres high with gale-force winds. We had drastically reduced sail and were just trying to hold our position as well as possible. The engine began to overheat and we realised that there was a broken coolant hose. Steve was violently sea-sick and in no state to offer much help. More worrying than the weather was the condition of my father. He had taken to his bunk and was clearly very weak indeed. I knew that my dad would never have lain down unless he was literally unable to raise himself. I was now skippering a boat with a broken engine and both of my crew effectively out of action. I was seriously worried and we were being pushed to the limit. The seas were such that going ashore was not an option. It is far safer to maintain a distance from land in such circumstances, so we simply had to ride it out as best we could.

I managed to have a word with Dad and, after a while he found the strength to have a go at the engine, repairing the damaged hose. He knew his boat well and was, as always, a brilliant fixer. Then he went straight back to his bunk, pale and exhausted. I desperately wanted to find a safe harbour, but was not confident enough to try for any of the small harbours marked on the chart in those conditions and with no local knowledge. I discussed it with Dad and he remembered that one of these had a safe approach. I set a course for it and, after several hours, motored quietly in between the navigation buoys. It was about 5 a.m. and, once moored up, we just slept. I had been five days at sea, fighting against dreadful conditions, with no sleep and no change of clothing. I had almost reached the stage of just letting go of the tiller and giving up. When we eventually awoke, the relief was palpable. My father had been drifting in and out of consciousness for the last few days, but now seemed better and he wouldn't hear of seeing a doctor. Steve had also recovered and, more than anything, we were all desperately hungry.

The port only consisted of a small scattering of scruffy buildings and we were delighted to find that one of them was a café. Inside, through the thick fog of steam and cigarette smoke, we saw huddles of rough-looking fishermen all shouting and gesticulating in machine-gun conversation, as only the Spanish do. We were made welcome by the owner, a large cheerful woman with dyed red hair and, without asking, were given large beers. There was no menu, but all the fishermen were tucking into a thick fish stew, so that was what we ate – and it was delicious. With our batteries charged and our spirits lifted, we completed the passage without incident and safely delivered *Jolie Fille* to her berth in the marina at Altea. I sometimes wonder what would have happened if I had allowed my father to sail her alone.

My parents enjoyed visiting the boat in Spain again and, about eighteen months after the eventful delivery voyage, they were driving back to the UK through France. They checked into a hotel in Blois, in the Loire Valley and, in the middle of the night, my mother became worried about Dad. He had chest pains and was in distress. She rang the night manager who immediately called an ambulance which rushed him off to the local hospital. There he was made comfortable and subjected to all kinds of tests. My brother and I flew out from England and we were told by the doctors that dad would need to have heart by-pass surgery urgently if he was to survive. The surgery was to be carried out at the nearby Tours hospital which was larger and had all the necessary facilities. The operation went well and, before long, he was on the road to recovery. I remember that he told me he hadn't felt so good for ages and he was full of praise for the team that treated him. It amused him when they insisted that he drank a small bottle of red wine every day with his evening meal, saying that it was an important part of his medication. 'You wouldn't get that in Lincoln County Hospital', he said.

Bizarrely, I think he actually enjoyed his stay in that French hospital and we were all relieved that he had recovered so well. However, the doctor took us to one side and asked us when he had had his heart attack. As far as we knew, he hadn't had one, but the doctor was most insistent saying that they were certain that he had – maybe a year or two before. Then I remembered how ill he had been on the boat passage to Spain and it all fell into place. In those chaotic few days at sea, I just hadn't realised how close he had come to death. In any case, there was nothing we could have done in the circumstances and, as ever, my dad had just suffered in silence, survived and then got on with his life.

Over the next few months, he started to find breathing more difficult and it was apparent that the years of working with dust, soot and asbestos had taken their toll. There soon came a time when he was more or less confined to a chair and his bed and he was given oxygen. One day in February 1994 I spoke to my mother by phone from Nottingham and she told me he had been taken into Lincoln hospital so I drove over to visit him. I sat by his bedside and he told me that he had been proud of me when we sailed together. I was moved beyond words. He then told me that he was not afraid of death – he was only sad to be leaving us behind.

On 26th February 1994 my dad died peacefully. He was a man of few words who always did his best. I still miss him and I am reminded of the words attributed to that statesman of ancient

Greece, Pericles, who said, 'What you leave behind is not what is engraved in stone monuments, but what is woven into the lives of others'.

We all rallied around my mother and, as always, she coped in her strong quiet way. She wanted to remain in the family home, even though it was larger than she needed. It held such happy memories for her and she busied herself cooking, cleaning and gardening. By that time, my sister had four children, my brother had two young girls and all of them doted on their granny. Their visits were a great consolation to my mum as she slowly came to terms with living alone after more than forty years of marriage.

I too was alone. I had no wife and children to console me and, even before the death of my father, was in a state of turmoil about where I was heading. I was distraught and yet seemed to have no answer except to keep on working hard as usual and going through the motions of everyday life. I remember, one Saturday, I was working alone in the warehouse and I climbed a high ladder to pull out a roll of fabric. I was careless and I tugged hard at the end of the polythene wrapping which suddenly came away in my hand. I lost my balance and found myself falling. I landed flat on my back and banged my head hard on the floor about two inches from a steel stanchion bolt. I lay there for a while and I think I must have been concussed. I realised that there was no blood and, although my head was throbbing and my back was painful, I was okay. It had been a close call. I was forty-three years old and I suddenly felt very lonely and vulnerable. Lying there on the cold concrete floor, I just cried uncontrollably as the grief of losing my father poured out of me.

Nineteen

Odyssey

The reason why I had been able to take over the helm of *Jolie Fille* on that nerve-racking passage from France to Spain was that, years before, I had qualified as a yacht skipper by studying for a RYA (Royal Yachting Association) Yachtmaster Certificate. The process began when I decided, with a group of friends, to take up cruising rather than dinghy sailing. We began by going for a couple of weeks flotilla sailing in the Greek Islands. Joining a flotilla is a fantastic way to start learning and all you need is a little sailing experience and maybe a grasp of basic seamanship. It's very safe because you are sailing in the company of other boats under the guidance of an experienced crew in a lead boat.

There is a skipper in overall command, typically helped by an engineer to assist with any technical or mechanical issues and a hostess to deal with the logistics of where to eat out ashore, where to obtain water, provisions and so on. The skipper runs a briefing each morning to go over the charts, discuss the day's sailing, the weather and sea conditions and any potential hazards. As you gain confidence and skill, you are given more freedom. Of course you may simply wish to follow the lead boat the whole time but, once the skipper sees that you are able, he or she will allow you to sail off and meet up in, say, two days time at a certain harbour or anchorage. You are always in radio contact so, if you get into difficulty, help is always at hand.

I had never been to the Greek Islands before but I immediately fell in love with the area. There are several thousand islands and islets in the Aegean and Ionian Seas, of which only 227 are inhabited, so the scope for sailing is huge. I could happily spend years sailing in these warm blue waters, dropping anchor in secluded bays for a swim and mooring up by waterside tavernas for visits ashore. There is no better way of exploring the islands than by boat. Indeed, some remote coves cannot be accessed any other way. The people of the islands are generally very friendly and they enjoy nothing more than sharing their timeless way of life with strangers.

After a couple of flotilla holidays, I wanted to have the freedom to charter a yacht without the constraints. My pal Stobart felt the same and so we both studied for our RYA Yachtmaster Certificates. This was just a shore-based qualification but, coupled with the practical experience at I.C.C. and on the flotilla holidays, it would allow us to charter yachts anywhere in the world. Thus, we found ourselves going to night school every week studying safety at sea, meteorology, maritime law, buoyage, lights, signalling, navigation and so on. We both enjoyed it immensely and, once completed, we couldn't wait to start our adventures.

We had no problem recruiting crews and so, every year, usually in June or September, avoiding the busy holiday season, we would spend time cruising around the Greek Islands. Initially, there were two boats, skippered by Stobart and me and then a third boat was added, skippered at different times by either Colin Elliot, a Nottingham property developer, or Dave (known as JLD – for reasons I won't mention) who bore a striking resemblance to Yasser Arafat. These boats were named by us as Blue, Green and Red simply because, when chartering, it's easier than remembering the real names of each vessel. My boat was always Green Boat. It certainly made radio communications simpler.

Typically, we would charter yachts between forty and fifty feet in length and these would be capable of sleeping eight adults. We, however, rarely took more than five to avoid the nightmare of big hairy snoring blokes having to share cabins and berths. We had reached an age when we valued our personal space.

By the way, on that subject, a few years later, when Stobart was about to be married, a bus-load of guys went over to Boulogne with the dual purpose of having a stag weekend and buying all the drink for his forthcoming wedding reception. We stayed in a small hotel and shared twin rooms to save money. Gordon the Tailor drew the short straw and shared with Jimbo, who was famous for insomnia, opening and closing windows and intermittent thunderous snoring. Over coffee and croissants the following morning, I said, 'Morning, Gordy. Did you have a good night?'

He rolled his eyes and replied with a sigh, 'It was like sleeping with a bison!'

The first sailing area we explored was the Saronic Gulf and the coast of East Peloponnese. This included the beautiful islands of Poros, Hydra and Spetses and south as far as Monemvasia on the mainland. I remember the first time we sailed into Hydra. The small sheltered harbour sits in a natural amphitheatre surrounded by the ancient town. There are no motor vehicles on the island except for a couple of rubbish trucks and so the only means of transport are mules, donkeys and water taxis. Then as now, the island lives principally from tourism, especially day-trippers from Athens who arrive by ferry or hydrofoil.

The picturesque port is well-served by bars and tavernas and I remember sitting outside a harbour front bar one warm afternoon. An old wooden trading boat had arrived from Athens with a full load of all kinds of supplies for the island. Immediately next to the bar ran a narrow stone alleyway which ascended steeply into the back of the town. The alley was just wide enough for two mules to pass each other and, seemingly from nowhere, there appeared a string of mules queuing to be loaded from the boat. From the bowels of the small ship appeared bags of cement, bricks and concrete blocks, all unloaded by hand. These were carefully strapped onto the waiting mules which were then driven between the bar tables and up the narrow alley. There followed boxes of canned food, fruit, tools and hardware, all taken away by mule. I remember thinking that this scene must have been acted out in exactly the same way for centuries. I could have watched them for hours – in fact, I believe I did.

Leonard Cohen, the musician and poet, had a little house in Hydra and he used to spend a lot of time there in the sixties with his lover and muse, Marianne Ihlen. She was immortalised in his song 'So Long, Marianne'. It must have been a very different place then but even now, especially when the tourist boats leave, there is a real magic about it.

In 1991, we approached Hydra from the north and, as usual, when approaching a harbour or anchorage, I studied the pilot book, which is a mine of useful information. As well as giving radio frequencies and a brief description of the facilities, it shows a small detailed chart of the approach, the harbour itself and any hazards to look out for. In Hydra Port there are berths for visiting yachts but it is invariably very crowded so you have to jostle your way in as best you can. There is also a small area at the western end which is reserved for small caiques and fishing boats. In the pilot book, there is a warning not to enter that area because, over the years, fishermen have lost chain in there and dumped old fishing tackle and other debris.

The usual way of mooring a boat in a busy harbour is to reverse towards the quay having dropped an anchor from the bow (front) of the boat. As you reverse in, you pay out the anchor cable and, having secured the stern (back) to rings or bollards, you tighten up the anchor cable to hold the boat tightly and prevent it from banging into the harbour wall in a swell. When the time comes to leave, you simply let go the stern lines and gently haul up the anchor cable to pull the boat out from its mooring. Whilst in the mooring, fenders are positioned along the sides of the yacht to act as cushions against other boats.

Green Boat and Blue Boat were moored up successfully and, after some time, Red Boat appeared, skippered by JLD. Despite the warnings in the pilot book and the advice of the two other skippers, he merrily dropped anchor in the fishing boat area and reversed in to secure to the quay. At the time JLD was wearing a Horatio Nelson outfit which caused a certain amount of interest in the town. I still have a photograph of him standing on the harbour wall at Hydra staring fixedly out to sea as if scanning the horizon for Napolean's navy.

We had a wonderful short stay and, when it was time to leave, Blue and Green Boats respectively slipped their moorings smoothly and began to head out of the harbour. As I looked round, I saw Red boat lurching violently at her cable. The anchor was stuck fast under something very solid and JLD's solution was to 'take a run at it'. This was not wise and it resulted in the electric windlass being bent and almost torn from its mountings. This caused an electrical fault and resulted in anything made of metal on the boat becoming live. Not only were they stuck fast amongst a tangle of fishing boat paraphernalia, but every time any member of the crew tried to handle a cable or steel rigging or guard rails, they received a good old electric shock. They were dancing around like dervishes while their clueless skipper shunted the boat to and fro' in a vain attempt to cut loose.

Amidst desperate talk of ditching the anchor with all the resulting expense and inconvenience, one voice of calm prevailed – that of one of the crew, Chris. He was a Nottingham solicitor who was new to our group. Clever, well-read and a tough ex rugby player, he was also more than a little eccentric. Realising that the boat was going nowhere fast and that skipper JLD was a lunatic, Chris dived over the bow of the yacht and into the tangle of ropes, chains and harbour debris. The water was about four metres deep and, every time he handled the chain it delivered a jolt to him. The anchor was well and truly wedged but he was fearless and, after a lung-bursting two or three attempts, he managed to free it. He was the hero of the day. We, on Green Boat, had been standing by, but were relieved to see them finally free and on their way.

There had been something approaching a mutiny and so, on subsequent trips, the gung-ho JLD was replaced as skipper of Red Boat by Colin Elliot, who was better qualified and displayed a little more common sense. However, the boat was now dubbed 'The Plague Ship' and, apart from Chris, the crew of Red Boat were into playing backgammon at every opportunity and were gambling serious money.

We all sailed to the island of Spetses and each moored to an old wall fringed by sharp rocks in the shelter of Cape Fanari, at the southern end of Spetses Town. It is an area simply known as The Old Harbour and we used long mooring lines to keep clear of the rocks, so it meant taking to our inflatable tenders to go ashore. The dinghies were always a source of amusement because, whenever we needed them to go to and from the shore, there was a fair chance that some bright spark would end up in the drink. We did have a tendency to overload the tenders so I suppose transporting five big clumsy men who have been a little over-enthusiastic with the drink always risked trouble.

Spetses, like the other islands of the Sporades, is delightful. Unlike Hydra, there are motor vehicles, but horse-drawn carriages are also widely used as taxis. Some of us used to hire motorcycles whilst on the islands, which allowed us to explore inland, often just on dirt roads. We were always getting lost. Road signs are few and far between and, to us, virtually illegible anyway. I remember once asking a toothless old shepherd for directions and, whilst we seemed to hit it off, having a very long and friendly conversation, I didn't understand a single word after the greeting of 'Kalimera' and, although I nodded and smiled a lot, was more confused than ever.

However, the nice thing about an island is that, if you keep going straight ahead, you eventually reach the coast road which you follow round until you reach somewhere you recognise. Chris was in that very situation on the tarmac coast road and he found himself following a rickety old truck. On a bend, past the truck, he saw a grass snake looping its way across the tarmac and, sadly, the truck ran over the poor creature. Chris stopped, picked up the dead snake and put it in his knapsack.

The following day, after buying provisions, all three boats set sail southwards, hugging the coast, until we found a large deserted bay where we dropped anchor. There we swam, tried to catch fish and went ashore to explore the beach and shoreline. We collected wood and, in the evening we lit a fire on the beach and had a barbecue. When German Kurt started to cooked succulent steaks, Chris produced the snake, washed it in the sea, prepared and cooked it. He and a few others had a go at eating it but, from what I saw, it was not a rewarding experience.

It was a beautiful moonlit night, the sea swished gently on the beach, the Red Boat crew set about their gambling and the rest of us chatted far into the night. It was so perfect that a few of the guys fetched blankets and pillows and slept on the beach until dawn. I returned to the boat and fell happily into my bunk.

There's something about sleeping on a boat at anchor that I find very therapeutic. The gentle motion and the soft tapping of ripples against the hull, even in windy conditions, the hum of the rigging and familiar creaks and rattles, have a strangely soothing effect. Most sailors will tell you that they are so tuned in to the noises of their boat that, if all suddenly goes quiet, they will wake up. A silent boat is potentially a boat that is drifting with wind and tide. The anchor might well be slipping and it could spell danger.

When we left the bay the following morning, we decided to make a race of it. The three yachts were anchored a hundred metres or so offshore. We agreed that the race would start with all men on land. At the blow of a whistle, we all had to run down the beach, climb into the inflatable tenders in a sort of 'Le-Mans Start'. We then had to row or paddle to our respective yachts, weigh anchor, set sail and race to an agreed finish line eight or ten miles away. Unbeknown to us, the dastardly Red Boat crew had partially deflated the other two dinghies. The spectacle of ten assorted idiots trying in vain to row two half-submerged and very floppy boats was a sight to behold. Needless to say, Red Boat were clear winners of the race.

The crew of Green Boat in the early 1990s was usually made up of five or six men. Apart from me, there was Smithy, Jimbo, Peter White and John 'Jockie' Wilson. We all got along well, pulling together when the sailing demanded it and each playing our individual parts in running the boat and entertaining each other. Jimbo, or 'Bilko', was in the habit of wearing a long dressing gown, with a silk cravat and slippers before turning in. Peter White fancied himself as a cocktail waiter, preparing weird and wonderful early evening drinks. Jockie Wilson loved creating lunchtime snacks and salads, even when the boat was listing at forty-five degrees. He was known as 'First Mate Vocal', due to his habit of repeating all my instructions to the crew when sailing.

Smithy was as skinny as whippet and liked nothing more than winching hard to tweak the sails. This line-up varied from trip to trip and, in 1994, Chris made his excuses with Red Boat and joined us. He immediately felt more at home on Green Boat and it was great to have him on board. He became our treasurer, or 'kitty man', raconteur, natural history consultant, diver, fisherman, hunter, poet and toastmaster – not necessarily in that order.

Again in the Saronic Gulf, we headed south down the Peloponnese coast to Monemvasia, an ancient fortified town founded in 583 A.D. It is perched on a huge rock, similar to the Rock of Gibraltar, jutting out into the sea and is only connected to the mainland by a two-hundred metre long causeway. It is the site of a powerful medieval fortress and a walled town containing several Byzantine churches and was historically an important maritime trading base. It has been attacked again and again over the centuries and has changed hands between Greeks, Venetians, Ottomans and others. Although when we last visited, it was almost deserted, Monemvasia has become a tourist attraction and a few small hotels and restaurants have appeared. We moored up in the small harbour in the shadow of the enormous rock and, for the next couple of days, explored, climbing to the plateau on the very top and eating in tiny restaurants by the old fortified walls.

When the time came to leave, our engine refused to start. We told our friends on the other boats to carry on without us, heading back northwards into the Saronic Gulf, while we tinkered with our motor. Nothing would do the trick but, luckily for us, a huge super-yacht had arrived and moored at the end of the harbour. The yacht was owned by a European prince and the six or seven full-time crew, who were all kitted out in smart white uniforms, included an English mechanic. He happened to walk past and seeing that we were struggling, offered to help.

He quickly established that it was a problem with the solenoid and we would need a new one. We gave him a beer and thanked him profusely. We immediately radioed the charter company and, after a few calls, they told us that they had ordered a new part and it would be delivered from Sparta, but would take a couple of days to arrive. We were stranded but, to be honest, there were worse places to be holed up and we had a relaxing few days enjoying our surroundings. Once fixed, we sailed off to rendezvous with our friends farther north.

There are plenty of challenges in sailing a forty-foot yacht and things don't always go to plan. Sometimes, however, just like skiing in fresh powder snow, the sailing is so perfect that you want it to last forever. One such time was when Green Boat was heading north east past Spetses and Hydra and back towards Poros in the Saronic Gulf. The sun was hot in a cloudless blue sky. There was a constant strong, steady breeze and the sea was friendly and calm. We set the boat up perfectly so that the big genoa foresail and the mainsail were taut. They were balanced so well that I hardly needed to touch the large stainless steel steering wheel to keep the yacht on course.

We set the auto-helm to the compass course and then left the boat to sail herself. She was heeling over and singing as she sped along. Now and again, I would wander forward to stand at the bow, holding on to the steel forestay, as the boat surged forward. The only sounds there were the hiss of the wind and the rush of the bow-wave. All we had to do was keep a good lookout but, in fact, there were no other boats to be seen. We had the universe to ourselves. We prepared a lunch of salad, bread and cheese and sat around the cockpit table, eating, chatting and drinking ice-cold rosé wine fresh from the fridge. This state of perfection lasted for two hours or more, but I believe the whole grinning crew and, indeed the boat herself, would have happily continued on that course forever.

Another group of islands we explored lay in The Ionian Sea, south of the Adriatic. The Ionian Islands, as they are known, lie just off the west coast of the Central Greek mainland, starting with Corfu in the north, down to Zante in the south. The other main islands in the group are Paxos, Lefkas, Ithaka and Kefalonia. They all have a rich history and I have great memories of sailing by day and then ghosting into little harbours to spend the evening and night ashore. One such place is the port of Gaios, the 'capital' of the small island of Paxos. Here, the Old Port sits in the shelter of a small islet, St Nicholas Island and you are able to moor up immediately facing Analipseos Square, in the centre of town. It's a perfect place in which to spend an evening eating and drinking at waterside tavernas and then walking just a few yards back to the boat.

It's surprising how, in the Greek Islands, even the most remote communities are able to come up with surprises. I remember our three yachts were once anchored in a secluded bay. There was a scattering of dwellings ashore and a few small fishing boats bobbing around a rickety wooden jetty. In the evening, we went ashore by dinghy and walked towards the sound of glowing lights and traditional music. Sure enough, there was a taverna, lively with the chatter of locals who made us welcome and, before we knew it we were eating tasty food and drinking too much. A couple of musicians played and things began to liven up. At about 10pm, Stobart began to nod off as usual, then stirred and said he would go back to the boat.

A thick-set fisherman with a huge moustache then took to his feet, crouched in front of one of the square wooden bar tables, took the corner in his teeth as if about to take a large bite from it and stood up straight. One of his companions did the same and both of them began dancing, Zorba-fashion, round and round to the music with the heavy tables raised and clenched firmly in their teeth. A waiter came and placed full glasses of beer on the tables as they twirled, I suppose as a reward for their efforts. Their strength was amazing. We tried the table-biting trick, but were barely able to move them a few inches along the floor.

We spent an enjoyable few hours with these happy people until, at last there were only three of our crew left. We wandered down to the old wooden jetty in the pitch dark, shining a little flashlight and, when we arrived we could see no rubber dinghy. We were debating what to do, where the last dinghy must have gone and so on, when we saw something moving under the planks beneath our feet. There, floating gently in the shallows, was a rubber dinghy containing a pair of oars and Stobart, rubbing his eyes and indignant at being woken up.

It became a sort of tradition that, on the final evening of a cruise, we would gather together all the left-over booze from each yacht and pour it into a large container – often a bucket – to make a punch. We would then all gather on one of the boats to partake of the resulting concoction as an 'aperitif'. We were thus assembled, fourteen salty dogs weighing down Red Boat and savouring the punch, when we realised that Angus was absent. He duly appeared from the depths of Blue Boat, which was moored alongside, freshly showered and dressed in his smartest shirt and white trousers. Now Angus was a large man, heavy, solid, with a bomb-like head and no neck. He walked along the quay onto the gangway of Red Boat and took two steps along it. The plank bent – and creaked – and then snapped like the jaws of a crocodile. He was instantly in the harbour, arms slapping the surface, submerging and then bursting forth with gasps and splutters. It was quite a party-piece and it was also no mean feat trying to fish eighteen stones of solid soggy humanity out of the harbour.

We were always sad when these trips came to an end but in the early 90s, there was a very dramatic finale. There were only five of us and we had chartered a magnificent 52-foot sloop from a marina close to Athens. The boat was immaculately finished in shining navy blue and featured all kinds of extras, like a bow-thruster for easy manoeuvring, a deep-freezer, air-conditioning – you name it. It must have been worth between one-and-a-half and two million pounds. We absolutely loved sailing her and we had a wonderful week. On the last full day, we had a leisurely lunch ashore and then only had to sail for a few hours back for a final night in the home port.

When we were an hour or so away from our destination, I decided to radio ahead for berthing instructions as usual. Alan was at the helm and I checked that he was happy. About two miles ahead of us was a large marker buoy which pinpointed a nasty submerged rock lying about a mile offshore. I gave him a course to steer, basically straight ahead between the buoy and the shore. There was a mile of open sea and all he had to do was follow another yacht on the same course a couple of miles ahead of us.

The wind had dropped and so we had taken all sail in and were motoring at six or seven knots. I made my way below and radioed the harbour master and the charter company. The charter manager asked if everything was alright with the boat. I told him it was perfect and that we would be arriving that evening ready for checking out in the morning. I then had a final look at my pilot book to check the approach to the harbour and made my way up the companionway. As I emerged on deck, the first thing I saw, no more than fifty feet ahead of us, was a very large marker buoy. I just about managed to say to Alan, 'What the...?', when there was a deafening crash and we were all thrown forwards. I instantly knew it was serious. The boat's deep heavy keel, probably alone weighing a couple of tons, was firmly wedged on the rock. We were stuck fast.

We were all uninjured so I positioned everyone at the very stern of the boat and, after a few attempts, managed to power off the rock. We were afloat, but water was coming into the saloon. In short, we were sinking. We switched on all pumps in an attempt to stay afloat and I then had a quick decision to make. Should I head straight for the shore about a mile away, or should I try to get her home, which would take at least an hour. Ashore, there was only a deserted beach, so driving in there would have meant the vessel lying on her side with possibly no easy way of reclaiming her and no immediate help on hand.

I decided to head for the home port and I found that, with all electric pumps working and maintaining a steady speed ahead, we were able to keep the flow to a minimum. I went below to check the situation. The floorboards were afloat, which meant the bilges were completely full of seawater. More seriously, the saloon table, which was located directly above the position of the keel, was sloping forwards at a jaunty angle. This told me that the keel had received such a bash that it had moved and damaged the boat's hull.

I returned to the radio and again called the charter manager, this time telling him to forget my previous message. Things had changed. I apologised, explained the situation and he said he would have a team standing by to help when we docked. I asked the crew to pack their bags and make sure that we were as prepared as possible for our arrival. Dusk was beginning to fall when we motored into harbour. We were quickly directed to where a large crane was positioned and there a diver was waiting to position long slings underneath our boat. We quickly threw our bags ashore and, before we knew it, the fifty-foot yacht was hanging in the air. I must say that the entire operation was extremely slick, with no time wasted. This meant that there was little or no damage to the interior fittings or electrics. The structural damage was, however, another matter. Once out of the water, we were able to see that the keel had indeed been hit with enough force to tilt it backwards and there was a crack showing where it joined the hull.

The manager had booked the five of us into a small nearby hotel where we showered and had a meal before bed. Before we flew home the following day, I had to file an accident report with the port police along with the Greek owner of the beautiful yacht we had just crashed. Never have I been more embarrassed. I couldn't apologise enough and I could feel his anguish. Nevertheless, both he and the charter manager were more than gracious in the circumstances. They shook my hand and consoled me, saying that it wasn't the first time a boat had hit a rock and it wouldn't be the last. We were well insured but that wasn't the point. It was the best boat by far that we had ever chartered and we had damaged it. The decision to make the dash back to port had turned out to be the right one, but the whole experience gave me nightmares for months afterwards.

Twenty

Yo-Ho-Ho!

There were a few years when we expanded our horizons into Turkish waters, collecting our charter yachts from Bodrum in the Gulf of G. Twenty five years ago, the port of Bodrum had not yet experienced the full onslaught of mass tourism. Yes, there were some hotels and there were the traditional wooden gulets, based on ancient trading boats, that had been adapted to accommodate tourists. I remember Jim Fisher from Red Boat recommending that I go to a traditional barber down one of the back-streets for a shave. I found the place and joined the handful of locals waiting. The shop was buzzing with conversation, full of cigarette smoke and the walls were covered with framed certificates of barbering excellence so, clearly, I was in good hands.

When my turn came, I was seated, lathered up and the cut-throat razor was stropped for action. I must say I was a little nervous but I need not have worried. The man was a true artist. The blade flashed and scraped and, before I knew it I was as smooth as silk. Then any stray bristles were singed with a burning taper, lotion was dabbed, talc was puffed and I was towelled down. He proceeded to pummel and massage my stiff neck and shoulders, then my arms and hands, pulling each finger one by one. I paid the equivalent of one pound and came from the shop feeling twenty years younger. I'm a big fan of Turkish barbers.

From Bodrum it's only a short sail eastwards along the Gulf of Gökova to a place called Cökertme, set in an open bay, which offers a useful overnight anchorage. No sooner had we dropped anchor, than a speedboat headed towards us from a beachside restaurant. 'Hello Misters – Welcome!', the driver shouted. 'You want eat with Captain Ibrahim tonight?'

'Yes, please, will 8-o'clock be alright?'

'No problem - how many persons?'

'Fifteen.'

'Okay – we will collect you.'

Sure enough, just before eight, the boat returned and shuttled us all ashore to Captain Ibrahim's Restaurant where we feasted for hours on delicious Turkish mezes and then a choice of fresh fish or steak or goat. We sampled the local aperitif, an anise-flavoured hooch called raki as well as the local rough wines and beers. The neat raki was so strong that Peter Crisp from Blue Boat refilled his Zippo lighter with it and it worked perfectly.

The meal was usually accompanied by a few local musicians playing odd-looking instruments – a simple bowed fiddle, a bağlama, which is like a lute, a nagara drum and a zurna, a reed instrument. The highlight of the evening was when Captain Ibrahim leaped into action dressed as a Turkish pirate, complete with high sea-boots, billowing shirt, doublet, a rakish hat, fake beard and an eye-patch. He carried a cutlass and wore a pair of pistols in his belt and he proceeded to whirl and bound, flourishing his cutlass and firing his pistols into the air with deafening bangs and plumes of white smoke. The Captain doesn't do things by halves. The whole evening, including all food and drink, entertainment and water transport, was ridiculously cheap. We were asked if we wanted to return for breakfast before sailing the following morning. We accepted and were again collected by boat. Once ashore, we were treated to a huge breakfast of bread, eggs, yogurt, honey, fresh orange juice, tea or coffee. We ate our fill and the bill came to the equivalent of 50 pence per person.

I remember on another visit to Captain Ibrahim's, he had procured a camel which you could ride up and down the beach. George, from Blue Boat, took a shine to the camel and insisted on riding it to and fro facing backwards. We passed a happy week exploring the rest of the Gulf of Gökova, spending the nights moored up in lovely sheltered bays like the one at Karacasogut. I remember entering the bay for the first time. There were two restaurants ashore, each with its own wooden jetty. As we cruised round the headland we saw the figure of an old lady, dressed all in black, waving the end of a hosepipe and shrieking for all she was worth. Naturally, we headed straight for her jetty, lured by the promise of fresh water for our tanks and a meal in her restaurant. Top of the menu was roast kid (goat, not child) which they cooked for hours over hot embers buried in an earth pit oven. It was tender and delicious.

There came a time when our travels took us to the Spanish island of Ibiza. We chartered boats from the marina in Santa Eulària and, over a few annual visits, explored the coast of the whole island from Portinatx in the north to Salinas in the south and then on to Formentera, the island strung out to the extreme south. Just off the north-west coast is the tiny private island of Tagomago. Here, we anchored in the shelter of cliffs, in perfectly clear water and went by dinghy to stone stairs leading up to a small bar/restaurant for lunch. There were two or three other visiting yachts but it was an idyllic place to pass a few hours.

The sailing is excellent around Ibiza but, I must say, the most memorable times are the times spent ashore enjoying long lunches and magical evenings. Two of our favourite haunts were at Las Salinas beach in the south. The Malibu Beach Bar sits behind the long sandy beach and we used to anchor in the wide open bay before swimming ashore or taking the dinghy in and enjoying long, leisurely lunches on the terrace.

Sailing southwards, the island of Formentera was a real pleasure. In the sixties and seventies it had been the haunt of a few hippies and local fishermen but, when we dropped anchor in the nineties, there were quite a few other yachts, as well as one or two ferries delivering day-trippers from Ibiza. There is a huge bay of perfect turquoise, fringed by miles of soft, white sand. It's more like a scene from the Caribbean than Europe and the water is warm and shallow, so yachts must anchor half a mile or so from the beach. It was perfect for swimming. On the beach is a restaurant called *Juan y Andrea*, which is expensive but superb. If you stood on the deck of your yacht and raised your arms, a boat would be sent from the restaurant to take you ashore. Chris Soar and I preferred to swim it, carrying a shirt and towel in a waterproof bag and I still treasure the memory of walking out of the crystal sea to enjoy a superb meal in paradise with good friends.

Leaving Formentera, heading back along the south-western coast of Ibiza, we sailed the narrow strait between the 400 metre high mystical rocky islet of Es Vedrà and the shore of the main island. Heading northwards, we at last reached San Antonio (Sant Antoni) and moored up in the large marina for a couple of nights. On the surface San Antonio is, it must be said, a little on the raucus side, aiming to please the young clubbers and revellers who throng to the island in the summer season.

However, on the outskirts of town, looking westwards out to sea there is a row of beach clubs, one of which is the famous Cafe del Mar and, for anyone who enjoys Chill music, it really is worth a visit. I say *is* – but I really mean *was*, because the place where we used to sit overlooking the shore, watching the sunset whilst sipping lumumbas, has been replaced by a large modern edifice – all glass and stainless steel. The slightly bohemian clientele and wandering fire-juggler have also been largely ousted by kids on a mission and it's all rather frantic. Even the chill music seems to have more of a persistently loud throb. Okay, it's my age.

I was living with Gilly and Stobart was married to Tracey. The girls weren't especially keen on wrestling with a sailing boat, so we decided to try our hand at power-yachting. We chartered a thirty-six-foot, twin-engine sport boat in Croatia and set about exploring the Dalmatian Islands. The boat was sleek and fast, perfect for two couples, with comfortable cabins and space for sun-bathing. I must point out that, in the world of sailing, taking up power boating is the equivalent of a Roman Catholic turning to voodoo, so we were a little apprehensive. As it turned out, however, the week we chose for our initiation could not have been more fortuitous.

There was virtually no wind the whole time, so a sailing yacht would have been wasted and we would have had to resort to chugging around under motor at five or six knots. In the event, we had an exhilarating top speed of thirty-six knots and were able to cruise all day at twenty-five. We could cover more ground and were able to decide on a lunch stop on one island before speeding off to spend the night on another, forty or fifty miles away. The boat had a shallow draught, with no deep heavy keel to worry about and so we were able to edge into the shallow waters of secluded coves and beaches.

It meant that we visited quite a few islands as well as interesting places on the mainland. We wandered from the magnificent Dubrovnik in the south and zig-zagged our way through the islands to the north. I have happy memories of spending time on the long, narrow island of Hvar. The port is so picturesque and we found lovely restaurants serving superb seafood. It was a wonderful, atmospheric setting and the people were very welcoming. The other really memorable place was Trogir on the mainland, not far from Split. It is a UNESCO World Heritage site. The ancient town is actually set on a small island linked by bridges and it dates back to the third century B.C.

Like many Mediterranean towns, it has been fought over and conquered by many different factions over the centuries. It has 2300 years of continuous urban tradition, influenced by Greeks and then the Romans. It has been sacked by the Saracens, protected and ruled by the Venetians for almost four centuries, ruled by Napoleon, absorbed into the Habsburg Empire, annexed by Italy, made part of Yugoslavia and so on, until it finally became part of modern Croatia in 1991. It really is worth a visit and I know I'm biased, but the best way to arrive there, in my opinion, is by boat.

To beat the gloom one winter, we decided to have a sailing holiday in the Caribbean. As well as Gilly and me, there were three other couples including Stobart and Tracey so, to be comfortable, we needed a fairly large yacht. I managed to book a spacious catamaran in the British Virgin Islands in January. It was the first time I had sailed outside Europe and I couldn't wait. We flew to Antigua and then took a ferry to the largest island, Tortola to collect the boat. I had raced small catamarans long before, but this was something else. It looked huge when we first saw it with lots of deck space and 'trampolines'- stretched netted areas between the two hulls – ideal for sun-bathing. There were, what looked like staircases down the back of each hull for easy swimming off the stern. A really spacious cockpit area with ample seating and glass doors lead into a superb saloon with a large round dining table, a state-of-the-art galley and an arc of windows giving good views of the surroundings. Each hull contained two double suites with large beds and shower rooms, so effectively we had four self-contained luxury suites. We were speechless. I remember we arrived at sunset and I have never seen one like it. The orange-red ball of the sun was huge and it fell like a disc of molten copper into a bath full of ink. We couldn't wait to start the adventure.

Before being let loose with the lovely catamaran, we were given a very useful briefing and I remember being warned about feeding fish. The marine life is wonderful in that part of the world and we were looking forward to snorkelling. Apparently, it's never a good idea to feed the fish because, some species in particular, work themselves up into something of a frenzy and fail to differentiate between tasty snacks and bits of human anatomy.

I loved the names of the islands: Tortola, Scrub Island, Salt Island, Cooper Island, Norman Island, Mosquito Island, Beef Island, Ginger Island and the Cays, or bays: Frenchmans Cay, Nanny Cay, Sea Cow Bay, Soper's Hole, Fat Hog's Bay, Brandywine Bay and so on. Sailing through the Sir Francis Drake Channel towards Dead Chest or Fallen Jerusalem, you could easily imagine being chased by Blackbeard or Captain Morgan.

We walked along perfect white beaches fringed by palms and anchored in turquoise bays. There were rickety wooden bars serving Pusser's Navy Rum (originally produced for the Royal Navy pursers) and waterside restaurants dishing up lobster or fish chowder. At the north-eastern end of the islands, we sailed around Neckar Island, the private domain of Sir Richard Branson, before heading back south-west to a feature known as The Baths, on Virgin Gorda, where huge smooth grey rocks sit like basking hippos in perfectly clear warm water. We anchored close in and swam ashore, taking our time to wade and wallow in these perfect rock-pools.

Not all of my expeditions were quite so exotic and, in August 1989, Stobart, Jockie Wilson and I chartered a 33-foot ketch from Starcross near Exmouth in Devon to cruise the South Devon coast. We navigated our way out of the estuary, carefully using the navigation buoys and channel markers to avoid running aground. As we approached the mouth of the estuary, we were confronted by a fleet of fishing trawlers, all decked out with bunting and crowded with the friends and families of their crews. They were returning from the annual Brixham Trawler Race and they were in high spirits, sounding fog-horns and claxons, singing and cheering as they rode the waves. We were headed towards Brixham from where they had come. The happy crews raised glasses and waved as we bounced our way through their wakes.

Having crossed Torbay, we moored for the night in Brixham Marina. Brixham still has an active fishing fleet and a commercial fish market so there is a healthy mix of tradition and tourism, giving the place its charm. There is a replica of Sir Francis Drake's ship, *Golden Hind* moored in the old harbour. Stobart's brother, Ralph, an artist, happened to live in the town with his family and he joined us the following day, for the next leg of our voyage south towards our old haunt, the Kingsbridge Estuary and Salcombe. Before we set sail southwards, we checked the weather forecast and there seemed to be an increased chance of stormy conditions in the following twenty-four hours.

As we made our way down the coast, the conditions slowly worsened and our radio told us that quite a serious storm was imminent. We made a decision to sail up the beautiful sheltered estuary of the River Dart and so we rounded the Mew Stone and motored our way into Dartmouth Harbour. In fact, we continued up the river to the village of Dittisham (which the locals pronounce 'Didshum'), sitting opposite to the estate of *Greenway House* where Agatha Christie used to live, now

191

managed by The National Trust. We moored to a visitor's buoy and promptly headed to the waterside pub, The Ferry Boat Inn.

While the storm raged out at sea, we reverted to type and became 'village idiots', wandering from pub to pub in Dartmouth and the nearby villages. The time came when Ralph had to leave us and Stobart offered to take him up river by dinghy to the village of Stoke Gabriel, from where he would make his own way back overland to Brixham. The little outboard motor was fixed to the rubber dinghy and, after saying our goodbyes, off went the two of them. Hours passed and there was no sign of a returning Stobart. Jockie and I didn't think too much about it until late afternoon, assuming the two brothers were simply enjoying each other's company in a village inn, but as dusk began to fall, we began to worry.

At long last, a very wet and bedraggled Stobart, slumped in the dinghy, drifted to our mooring. We hauled him aboard and interrogated him. He had made the cardinal error of failing to take a pair of oars with him. Sure enough, after he delivered his brother ashore, the outboard had failed and he was stranded. From Stoke Gabriel, he had half drifted and half waded, dragging the dinghy, making his laborious way back to Dittisham. That night, he slept like a baby.

After a couple of days, the storm at sea subsided and we were able to continue our coastal passage round Prawle Point to the Kingsbridge Estuary. Approaching this estuary from the sea is not to be taken lightly. Even experienced Salcombe fishermen treat the approach with care because of a feature simply known as The Bar. The safest line to take across The Bar is marked by transit posts ashore, which you keep in line as you make your approach. Even then, in certain conditions, with steep seas and at low tide, it is dangerous, if not impossible to enter. Many boats have foundered there and I had a close call myself when sailing a twenty-one-foot keelboat with friends from the I.C.C.

We were totally swamped, and hit the sand, but managed to recover, pump like hell and live to tell the tale.

It was a different story on October 27th 1916, when the Salcombe lifeboat William and Emma was launched to go to the aid of a stricken schooner that had gone aground at Lannacombe Bay. Fifteen men crewed her as she made it out over The Bar in a furious gale, led by Coxwain, Samuel Distin. When they arrived at the wreck, it became apparent that all the crew had already been taken off by using a rocket line from shore, so the lifeboat was not needed after all. All that remained was to get safely back home. The crew members were freezing cold and soaked through as they approached the notorious Bar, where huge angry waves were breaking.

They could have opted to row and sail all the way back to the safety of Dartmouth but, in the event, they decided to risk running The Bar. It was a catastrophe. The boat was instantly swamped as the storm smashed it down. When the wreckage was recovered, there were only two exhausted men still alive and clinging to the upturned hull, Eddie Distin and William Johnson. It is a testament to the bravery of the people of these coastal communities that a new crew quickly volunteered to man a replacement lifeboat and the coxswain of that boat was none other than Eddie Distin, one of the two survivors of the disaster.

Our last port of call before returning our ketch to Exmouth, was the delightful River Yealm. Approaching from the sea, the entrance is very difficult to spot as the estuary takes a sharp right turn just round Gara Point. Once inside, there is then a very narrow channel past a sand bar into the main body of the river and a safe mooring. We were moored just below the River Yealm Hotel, an imposing Edwardian building sitting high on the north shore reached by steep steps. I am told that the hotel is now closed and has been sold and re-developed for residential use but, in those days, it was presided over by a larger-than-life character called Thatch Wilson. We decided to pop up there to have a cooked breakfast on the terrace whilst taking in the stunning river views. We had a great breakfast of kedgeree, served by a young French waitress, neatly dressed in black and white.

On the north shore, lies the lovely village of Newton Ferrers and, on the opposite side is the quaint Noss Mayo, both of which have good pubs. We had a great time walking the riverside paths and dabbling in the shallows, but the time came when we had to set sail again and make our way back to Exmouth. The return leg of the trip was relaxing and, in contrast to the stormy interlude in Dartmouth, the weather treated us well as we returned the boat safely to its home mooring.

Twenty-One

Stand and Deliver

It crossed my mind that, given my enduring affection for boats and the sea, I might make a career out of delivering yachts. I had met one or two characters over the years who earned a living by moving boats for wealthy clients between say the Mediterranean and the Caribbean. I daydreamed about it now and again but, in the early summer of 1992, Stobart and I were asked by a mutual friend, Geoff, to move a 47-foot yacht for him from Corfu to Menorca. He and a business partner, Roger, had bought it in Gouvia, on the east coast of Corfu. The timing couldn't have been better because we had planned one of our usual three-yacht adventures around the southern Ionian Islands, starting and finishing at the port of Nidri on the island of Lefkas. At the end of the week-long cruise, the charter company wanted the boats back in Gouvia. It was an unbelievable coincidence, so Stobart and I offered to deliver two of the three yachts back to Gouvia over a couple of days. It suited us perfectly, because we would then be able to collect Geoff's new boat, *Moonwatch,* for passage to Menorca.

We said goodbye to our companions, who all flew off to the UK and we then motored off northwards in our respective boats, passing through the narrow Lefkas Canal and setting a course for the northern tip of the island of Paxos. There was only a gentle swell to the sea and winds were light, so we had no problem in managing our boats single-handed. We motor-sailed, that is we used our engines but hoisted mainsails for stability. Stobart took the lead and I followed. We made good progress and arrived in the sheltered port of Lakka in late afternoon. The village lies at the head of a sheltered bay at the northern tip of the island. We both dropped anchor in the pristine bay, Stobart collected me in his dinghy and we went ashore for a meal. I remember sitting at a quayside taverna with a couple of beers, watching the sun slowly setting.

We made an early start the following morning, quietly raising our anchors and, once more motoring in convoy. It was perfectly peaceful, apart from the gentle thump of the engine and there was no hint of a breeze. The surface of the sea was as smooth as a mirror and I followed a hundred yards or so in Stobart's wake. No sooner had we emerged into the open sea, setting a course for Corfu, than we were joined by a trio of dolphins who seemed to want to act as our pilots. It was pure magic and they played with us for almost an hour, scything through the turquoise water before eventually disappearing to find amusement elsewhere.

Following the Gulf of Corfu northwards, we arrived at Gouvia. Entering the bay, heading in towards the marina, we could make out low arched structures on the north shore. These are Venetian galley sheds, part of an arsenal built in 1716, where war galleys were stored and maintained to defend against the Ottomans. We moored up in the marina and checked both boats in with the charter company who were grateful that we had delivered them, saving them a job. We then met Geoff, his wife Jane and friend Roger, to be shown around *Moonwatch*, which was to be our floating home for the next couple of weeks. Geoff and Jane would not be sailing with us as they had business back in the UK, but Roger, the co-owner was looking forward to the forthcoming voyage. He had never sailed before, but was very keen to learn and to play with his new toy. The yacht was not brand new but she was in excellent condition and had been bought complete with a stock of quality wines and a pump-action shotgun hidden away for repelling pirates.

We wasted no time in provisioning and planning the first leg of our voyage, which was towards Valletta in Malta, where I had last been in 1966 with the Sea Cadets. The course was pretty straightforward, being a straight line across the Ionian Sea for about 400 miles in a south-westerly direction. The forecast was for unsettled weather and we had to prepare for heavy going as we left the channel between Corfu and Paxos. Towards evening, we reduced sail and made everything secure ready for a hard blow. Sure enough, the seas became steep and the wind increased in strength and there were heavy squally showers. Looking astern, we could see lightning flashes over Corfu. We worked a simple watch system between the three of us but it soon became apparent that Roger was succumbing to sea-sickness. He turned a very interesting shade of green and, whilst trying his best to continue to contribute, it became clear that Stobart and I would be doing the lion's share, leaving poor Roger to deal with his own issues, as it were.

Conditions worsened considerably as we progressed and we were stretched, trying to stay on course, whilst high waves battered us broadside on. It was uncomfortable to say the least, but Roger's condition seemed to improve and he became used to the wild motion of the boat. We learned that he had a passion for F.E.Bs (Full English Breakfasts) and so dramatic was his improvement that, by the third day, he was cooking an enormous fried breakfast for us all in the hot and steamy galley. Sea-sickness affects people in many different ways and, for some, it just hits them for a day or two and then subsides and they are as right as rain.

I am lucky in that, even the wildest motion has little or no effect. The exceptions are that, if I spend time below decks doing close work, studying charts for instance, there comes a point where I feel a little queasy and have to go out on deck for a look around. It also seems that 'awkward' following waves or swells from astern, not necessarily violent movements, may have the worst effect.

It's a known fact that Nelson, England's most famous sailor, suffered from sea-sickness. He wrote, in a letter to Lord Camden in 1804, *'I am ill every time it blows hard and nothing but my enthusiastic love for the profession keeps me one hour at sea.'* (in a letter on display at the Tunbridge Wells Museum to 2nd Earl of Camden to explain why his nephew had left HMS Victory just a few months after joining the Navy).

It was in these uncomfortable conditions that we had noticed a lone swallow circling our boat and it soon decided to settle on our rigging. When dusk fell, it flew into the saloon and settled on our book shelf, where it passed the night seemingly unaffected by our comings and goings. I can only imagine that it was exhausted and maybe had been blown off its migration course by the storm. We tried to give it water in a saucer but it just wanted to sleep. The following day, it flew out, perched at the masthead for a while, did a quick lap of honour around the boat and then disappeared off towards the horizon.

I remember that, with huge relief, we sighted the Fort St. Elmo light at half past midnight on Sunday and fought our way to Lazaretto Creek, near Valletta, arriving at around 3 a.m., having radioed ahead to the harbour authorities. Whoever we spoke to understood just how exhausted we were and gave us permission to simply drop anchor, leaving all formalities until the following day. We motored in, found a safe place and, with huge relief, anchored. We then poured ourselves a large tumbler of whisky each and raised a glass to our safe arrival, before collapsing into our bunks. We were all dead to the world until around eleven the next morning, when we reported to the harbour office. It had been thirty years or more since I was last in Valletta and the place had changed significantly. The Royal Navy now had no presence and tourism had become far more important.

After a day or so of relaxation and provisioning the yacht, we set forth on the next stage of our mission. We headed out of port, past the smaller island of Gozo and set a course for Sardinia about 400 miles away. We had a following sea with long, heaving waves, lifting and then stalling us as we reached each trough. It was uncomfortable. There was a haziness in the sky and a steady following wind as we progressed slowly under full sail. Out of the murky air, insects began to fall on the boat. There were huge crickets and all kinds of flying bugs, some dead, some alive, dropping on us accompanied by grass, twigs and a reddish dust. I guess there must have been an almighty storm somewhere in North Africa off to our south-west.

Sicily was somewhere over the horizon to the north-east of us and, after about 150 miles, we saw the high profile of the volcanic island of Pantalleria, which belongs to Italy and has played important strategic roles throughout history. There is an airfield at the northern end of the island and it played a significant part in the Second World War when the allies eventually invaded Sicily.

The going was a little tedious and we decided to amuse ourselves for a while by setting up a 'clay shoot' using the pump-action shot gun. We had a few empty wine bottles to dispose of, so we took turns at standing at the bow and throwing bottles as high as we could for the guys in the cockpit to shoot at. Instead of the usual two shots from a traditional gun, the pump-action, like those carried by American traffic cops, held five cartridges. So, if you missed the bottle in the air, you could still keep on blasting away at it until it sank. It wasn't the most eco-friendly way to pass an hour, but we enjoyed letting off steam to break the monotony.

The satellite navigation system on the yacht was not working properly. It was so temperamental that we simply had no faith in it and we were relying entirely on our own dead-reckoning skills, just using time, heading, speed and occasional compass bearings when we were in site of land or lights. It worked well and we were quite pleased with ourselves when Sardinia appeared directly ahead of us exactly as expected. We initially headed into the port of Cagliari in the south. We passed one night there but were charged a ridiculously high fee for mooring overnight by the most unpleasant and miserable official, so we couldn't wait to leave.

We sailed round the southern tip and then made our way northwards between Sant'Antioco and the tiny Isola di San Pietro. The waters here were crystal-clear and shallow, barely deep enough for us to navigate, so we proceeded very carefully until we arrived at the harbour of Carloforte. The following morning, we breakfasted ashore in the courtyard of a small hotel by the tree-lined harbour frontage. Afterwards, we wandered past a small shaded square by a church and there were long benches occupied entirely by old men, all chattering away, setting the world right as old men do the world over. We soon realised that they were simply passing the time while their women-folk were in church praying for forgiveness and, sure enough, when the church doors opened, out flooded the all-female congregation. . Early that Sunday afternoon, we left Carloforte and, as we sailed up the strait, we found ourselves amongst dozens of small boats racing each other. They were all lateen-rigged, using an ancient middle-eastern sail design like the Arab dhows on the River Nile. The single white wing-shaped sails looked so elegant and the crews shouted happy greetings to us as we passed.

I would have liked to spend more time on the little island but, sadly, we had a yacht to deliver and so, we now set a course eastwards for Menorca. This leg of the voyage was around 250 miles long and we again had to rely on dead-reckoning for navigation. All went well until we reached a time when we should have been within sight of the island. We had kept a close check on speed and heading by day and night but, just to make life difficult, a fog descended on us, greatly reducing visibility. We continued on track for another hour or so and there was still no sight of land.

It's tempting at sea, in these situations, to start milling around in circles in an ever more desperate attempt to find a landfall but we reasoned that, if anything, we had under-estimated our leeway. That is the sideways drift caused by wind and tides. We were pretty sure that we had travelled far enough but clearly the direction was wrong. We turned ninety degrees to port and held that course.

Within half an hour or so, directly ahead of us through the swirling fog, we saw a high cliff with a lighthouse perched on top. We knew immediately that it was Cap de Cavalleria at the very northern tip of Menorca. If we had not made the sharp turn, we would have missed Menorca completely and the next landfall would have been goodness knows where on the Spanish mainland. After eventually making our way round to our final destination, the small port of Addaya, we were met by co-owner Geoff, happy to be re-united with his boat.

Another friend from Nottingham, Nigel, bought a forty-two foot catamaran which was lying in Gibraltar. He had limited sailing experience but, having taken possession, he had paid an instructor to give him a crash course, putting him through his paces in the Bay of Algeciras and further into the Mediterranean. Nigel wanted to base the boat in Ibiza and he asked me if I would be interested in helping him sail it to its new home. He also had a mate, Len, a major in the U.S. Air Force who was keen to come along.

Before delivering the boat, the instructor was to take us on a short visit to Morocco as a final exercise for Nigel. We sailed across the Strait of Gibraltar and down the west coast of Spanish Morocco. I have only a vague memory of our overnight stay there but I do remember it was the Holy Month of Ramadan and it was the first time I tasted cous-cous. It was awful. It was grey, looked like wallpaper paste and tasted worse. Lurking in its depths were soggy lumps of matching grey, dubious-looking, boiled meat. I was not impressed but, fortunately, I have eaten cous-cous many times since and I love it. We ate in a 'traditional' Moroccan restaurant where we were entertained by a fat, rather clumsy, belly-dancer who clearly thought she was a heavenly temptress. If the food wasn't bad enough already, the dancer would have spoiled our appetites anyway.

The sailing instructor suggested that, before we leave, we should see the souk in Tetouan, just inland. He recommended that we hire a guide to help fend off beggars and dodgy traders and, as it turned out, this was good advice. Tetouan is known for its leather and the guide suggested that we should visit a traditional tannery. I remember walking through an arched doorway and into a wall of stench. The place was filthy and, in one corner, was a pile of cows' heads enveloped in a cloud of flies. The huge courtyard was a maze of sunken clay pits, each filled with reeking liquid. In some of the pits, men were thigh-deep, scraping and working skins. Other pits were filled with brightly-coloured dyes and sweating workers who dipped and soaked the leathers with blue and orange limbs. On the surrounding mud walls, there were wooden frames with skins stretched out to dry. It was a hive of activity but the sheer stink of dead flesh was so overwhelming, that I couldn't wait to leave. It sticks in my mind as the worst tourist attraction I have ever visited.

Once back in Gibraltar, Nigel, Len and I said goodbye to the instructor and prepared to sail for Ibiza. The plan was to break the journey roughly halfway at the port of Cartagena, about 250 nautical miles from Gibraltar. This first leg of the passage was superb. On the first day, we were joined by a large pod of dolphins. There were dozens of them arcing and speeding all around the boat. I remember sitting on the bow trampoline with my feet dangling and, each time we descended into a trough, my bare feet touched the water. Some of the dolphins were curious and playful, racing right between our twin hulls. One of them timed it perfectly and brushed my toes as they dipped into the sea. It was truly magical and they were as intrigued by us as we were by them. They rolled on one side to get a better look at us, exhaling with a whoosh as they breached. There was something in the eye contact and the breathing that I found fascinating. These were beautiful wild creatures but there was an undeniable bond. It's always a privilege to share time with these powerful, intelligent animals.

We used a standard watch system and I remember being alone in the cockpit on a perfect moonlit night. The boat was running on autohelm, under full sail in a gentle swell and there is nothing like silver moonlight on the sea. Looking aft, I could see the shimmer of phosphorescence in our wake. It was perfect. I looked at the inky sky and noticed, now and again, white shapes flying past our sail. I was lost in thought, wondering what sea-birds were doing there at night, when something big and heavy hit me on top of my head. I nearly jumped out of my skin. Then, floundering on the floor of the cockpit, I saw a large flying fish, with huge staring eyes and with fins elongated to form 'wings'. Once over the shock of being slapped on the head, I filled a bucket with sea-water and put the flapping fish in to show my crew-mates when they awoke.

Cartagena, in the region of Murcia, is one of the best harbours in the Western Mediterranean. It has, for centuries been of great strategic use, has a rich and varied history and is an important base for the Spanish Navy. We spent one night there and, the following morning, I chatted to an old man who was fishing from the quayside. I showed him the flying fish and he touched his lips with a 'good to eat – yum-yum' gesture so I presented it to him and he was delighted. We slipped out of Cartagena and set a course towards Ibiza, about 150 nautical miles to the north-east.

That night, I was again on watch alone whilst the other two slept peacefully in their cabins. It was another clear, moonlit night and the boat was sailing herself beautifully. I noticed on the horizon ahead a band of jet black cloud stretching from east to west as far as I could see. I had never seen anything like it, but conditions were perfect and we were sailing well. The black cloud came ever closer and I watched it with a mixture of curiosity and bafflement. What could it be? As I wondered, it grew very quickly into a monstrous, looming wall of blackness and suddenly, like a huge hammer, it struck the boat with enormous force.

I hadn't had the sense to reduce sail so the boat was at the mercy of the beast. Catamarans can be especially vulnerable to such impacts. Whereas a single hull boat will be knocked over by such a force and then, hopefully right itself, thanks to the weight of a heavy keel, catamarans sit rigidly on the surface and bits often just snap off. How nothing broke that night, I will never know, but clearly it was a strong and well-built vessel because we got away with it without even a torn sail.

The enormous bang and screeching wind woke my two friends instantly and, thinking we had had a serious collision, they both leaped on deck ready to abandon ship. We wrestled to reduce sail, get the boat under control and continue on course in very lively conditions. What we had experienced was a Line Squall. These are features associated with an advancing cold front and, believe me, once bitten, twice shy. I would certainly recognise one if I saw one again and would make preparations for the onslaught. It just goes to show that you never stop learning.

We took our time as we approached Ibiza and we passed to the south of Formentera. It was dark and we were relying on a series of lights from shore to confirm our position as we headed towards Ibiza town, taking care to avoid obstacles like the Isla Espardell. As darkness faded into a new dawn, we motored into Marina Botafoch, just away from the bustle of the town. The boat had been safely delivered to her new home.

Twenty-Two

Feel the Quality

It might appear that my whole life has been spent swanning around on yachts but, rest assured, in between the adventures, I had to seriously apply myself to earning a living. My little textile business was flourishing and there came a point in 1997 when the warehouse I was sharing with Simon was clearly not big enough for the two of us. While we helped each other as much as possible, we had kept our businesses separate, neither of us wishing to form a partnership. I was doing some business with another textile trader called Tony Dale and, the more we got to know each other, the more we felt that we would both benefit from working closely together. We had built up our respective enterprises in different ways but were roughly equal in terms of assets, so it seemed logical to pool our resources.

Simon and I parted company amicably. We gave up the warehouse and he moved to new premises out of town. Tony and I rented an office and larger warehouse backing on to the River Trent in Nottingham and formed a limited company. We tidied the place up, painted the walls and installed racking to store thousands of rolls of fabric. From the start, I made a concerted effort to expand the export side of the business to set us apart from other fabric traders operating in the UK. Finding new clients was like finding a needle in a haystack but, as time went by, we grew the business into a thriving enterprise.

The key to success was keeping costs under control by being willing to turn our hands to all aspects of the business. We would both unload the large truck-loads of textiles by hand, sorting and checking the quality and storing ready for sale. We would be telephoning around the world, buying and selling. Sample swatches had to be cut and parcelled off to clients. I tended to focus on the marketing side of things while Tony dealt with accounts and finance, but both of us shared the hard physical work of processing the orders and handling the heavy rolls of fabric.

Before we knew it we had a thriving business with a wide clientele in many different countries. The international business meant travelling widely, but always on the cheap to keep costs down. We would use budget airlines and ran an ad-hoc competition to find the cheapest hotel accommodation. While one of us travelled, the other would be holding the fort in Nottingham. I always liked the challenge of finding new customers in unexpected corners of the world, so I found myself travelling to Estonia, Latvia, Cyprus, Iceland, Finland and Russia, as well as the more accessible France, Germany, Belgium and so on. Our fixation on travelling as cheaply as possible sometimes led to interesting situations.

I remember once hiring a car to drive across the breadth of Finland in winter to see a particular client. I had booked the cheapest car possible and, when I arrived at the hire desk, I was told that the car allocated to me was a Smart Car. I had never driven one before. I'm quite tall and Smart Cars are tiny two-seaters, featuring dinky little wheels and what sounds like a lawnmower engine. There was barely room in it for me, my sample case and my suitcase so I was hunched behind the wheel like some kind of deformed ape.

Now, don't get me wrong, Smart Cars are just fine for young folk nipping around the city, but a few hundred miles across the middle of Finland in the gloom of their winter is an entirely different matter. Luckily, the car was fitted with winter tyres, which are compulsory in most Scandinavian countries, so there was little risk of skidding off the road. However, I felt every bump and pothole between Tampere and Punkaharju. When I eventually clawed my way out of the car at my destination, I was numb and couldn't stand up straight. I seem to remember selling plenty of fabric, so perhaps the client took pity on me.

Experience has since made me very wary of car rental companies, who generally seem to work on the principle that all of their customers are complete nincompoops. In fact, we *are* such nincompoops that, when we book a car, we don't bother reading the 28 pages of minute print informing us of all the extras and add-ons that will be applied to double or triple the quoted price.

I once arrived at Stansted Airport Car Rental Village, having pre-booked and pre-paid on-line. I had chosen the cheapest option, from the 'mini' category. At the hire desk, I was greeted by a youth with a pale face peppered with bum-fluff and topped by a haircut with an exaggerated gelled-up quiff. He wore a reluctant tie over a button-bustingly tight white shirt and a highly restrictive pair of black strides that were two sizes too small.

He started well, except he called me 'Mate' after each sentence, tried to sell me six different kinds of 'essential' insurance and offered every upgrade from sat-navs to ejector-seats. He tapped his keyboard ferociously and sucked his breath - and sighed, said 'Jast a minit, mate.' and disappeared into his office. He then reappeared, picked up the phone and began to talk to someone about whether the Peugeot was available. After a session of 'Hmms' and 'Haas' and 'Oh, reallys', he said, 'Do we

'ave anyfink?..Mmmm. We'll maybe aff to give 'im the Toyo-ah.'
And so it went on.

Clearly, he was struggling to locate a car for me. Bearing in mind it was the middle of winter, presumably low-season and I had booked a month previously, I wondered how he would manage in the peak of the holiday season. After flitting in and out of the back office to check with a mysterious Superior, he asked if a (what sounded like) Toyo-ah Collapso would be OK. My life was ebbing away and I said that anything with four wheels would be fine. He asked for my credit card to block off an amount for security and, after a few attempts, said the transaction couldn't be validated. In fact, he couldn't validate any of my cards (I only have two). So he fetched his Superior, who ambled out of his lair, looked at me as though I'd just crawled from under a stone and proceeded to talk about me as if I wasn't in the room. 'We'll need to see a u-il-i-y bill or a bank sta-ement from the gen-leman to confirm his I.D. Avverwise 'e carn'ave the car.' He turned round and waddled back into his office.

In short, the farce went on for almost an hour and I was on the point of telling them where they could stick their 'Toyo-ah', but I realised that, if I did, instead of paying the pre-booked price of about seventy pounds, it might end up being three or four hundred with another company. I managed to bring up a recent bank statement on my mobile phone. The youth glanced at it and said, 'Yeh, vat seems or-igh, mate.. I'll take ya ter yer car.'

On one visit to the Baltic States, I visited a few clients in Estonia and then wanted to see three more in Riga, the Capital of Latvia. In my wisdom, I decided that, if I hired a car, I would be able to drive there and back without an overnight stop. The return journey of 600 kms from Tallinn to Riga could be done in a day so I duly jumped into a fairly rough-looking hired Peugeot and off I went. Again, the car was fitted with snow tyres, which was fortunate because the weather worsened and, before long, I was driving in blizzard conditions. The road was mostly straight, mainly through dense forests and covered with sheet ice and drifting snow. Studded winter tyres are fantastic and gripping the road was not an issue. Visibility, however, was poor, so driving required intense concentration, hour after hour.

Despite everything, I made reasonable time and visited the customers as agreed. Then, business done, I had to face the long slog back to Tallinn in the same conditions. There was very little traffic, mainly just heavy trucks carrying huge logs but, just before I reached the border between the two countries, I saw a bright orange light swinging to and fro in the swirling snow. I slowed down and, as I drew close, I saw that it was a beefy-looking uniformed policeman, flagging me to the roadside. There were, in fact two beefy-looking policemen with a squad car from which officer number two was toting a radar-gun and they indicated that I should get out and sit in the back of their car. When I did, they slammed the doors shut and I was surprised to hear some kind of techno music pounding away and there was a very graphic girlie calendar hanging from the dashboard. The two burly Latvian officers spoke not a word of English and I spoke not a word of Latvian but, through grunts and sign-language, they informed me that I had been caught speeding in a built-up area.

I had noticed occasional roadside signs depicting the shape of a house but, in the blizzard, there was no sign of the real thing. It all looked like forest to me. Anyhow, seeing their useful-looking side-arms, night sticks and the pump-action shotgun clipped over the windscreen, I wasn't going to argue the toss. They wrote out an official-looking ticket with a sum of so many lats scrawled on it by way of an on-the-spot fine. I forget the amount, but I only had about half on me in lats and some more in euros. Latvia didn't start using euros until 2014.

It crossed my mind that these two might be con-men disguised as cops, but again, I wasn't in any position to question them. I emptied my pockets with a theatrical shrug, suggesting, 'That's all there is. Take it or leave it.' Fortunately, they took the lats, crossed out the first amount and re-wrote the ticket. After a finger-wagging, incomprehensible lecture on what I assume was the Latvian Highway Code, I was allowed to leave to continue my journey. Once back in Tallinn, I fell into my hotel bed, completely exhausted.

We were very proud of the way the business was developing because we had made a determined effort to find markets rarely explored by other small UK firms. Many other companies had any foreign connections, mainly importing cheap goods from China, but we were actually net *exporters*. I saw it as a personal crusade to trade abroad and I really wanted to find clients in Germany, the richest country in Europe. I had met an amiable German wholesaler at a trade show and he told me quite bluntly that I would never be able to sell into Germany because we were not competitive. That was red rag to a bull and, within two years, Germany was our biggest and most profitable market outside the UK. I just kept banging on doors and posting samples. I recruited a German commission agent called Oliver and the business steadily grew.

The next challenge was Russia, geographically the largest country in the world and stretching across eleven time zones. I attended meetings with trade delegations, approached The Chamber of Commerce, bought lists of potential Russian partners and so on, all without success. It was going to be difficult but, by chance, an Austrian contact gave me the name of a woman in Saint-Petersburg who, he suggested, might be interested in acting as a sales agent. Having no knowledge of the country or the language, we needed a Russian-speaking agent.

One thing led to another and, before long, we were working with Masha, our agent in Saint-Petersburg and Irina, who covered the Moscow area. Masha, in particular, became a good friend and I was made very welcome by her whole family whenever I visited.

Doing business in Russia is different. It is fraught with all kinds of dangers involving logistics, transport, customs and criminal scams. I soon learned whom I could trust and I was very careful about extending credit to customers. It takes an awful lot of patience to navigate through the peculiarly Russian ways of doing business but, despite one or two mistakes, I managed to do it. I found it very interesting just travelling around and meeting all kinds of characters.

The first time I visited, I stayed in a monolithic hotel of more than a thousand rooms. It was a throwback to Soviet times and from the outside it looked impressive , in a 1960s way. The spacious foyer and reception areas were equally magnificent, with plush carpets and plenty of gold paint and garish, in-your-face artwork. My room however, was a different kettle of fish. There was no plug in the bath, the tap water flowed an interesting shade of brown and there were mouldy squares where tiles had fallen off the bathroom wall. The tiny T.V. only received snow blizzards and the drab, ill-fitting curtains failed miserably to blot out the alternating red, blue and green floodlighting that nightly and brightly bathed the immense slab-fronted exterior of the building – and the interior of my room. It was like trying to sleep in a 70s disco. Duct tape had been applied to try to exclude window draughts and the carpet was incredibly sticky. Apart from that, it was lovely.

In the morning, I went down to the hangar-sized dining room for a buffet breakfast and was astonished at the food on offer. As well as the usual breakfast offerings of cereals, yogurt, eggs in all their forms and so on, there was soup, steamed broccoli, chicken drumsticks, several kinds of fish, trifles, and dozens of different sorts of puddings and cakes. But by far the best part of breakfast was the musical accompaniment. A woman of a certain age who bore a striking resemblance to Rosa Klebb, the Russian counter-intelligence agent from SMERSH in the original James Bond 'From Russia with Love' film, played an electric organ *very* loudly. Her grimly expressionless renditions of what were meant to be stirring patriotic martial numbers rendered the breakfast experience tense and farcical. It's hard to focus on which cheese to have with your pickled herring when somebody like that is banging out a strident Red Army march on a 1950s electric organ. As I teetered my way to my table with a loaded tray, trying not to goose-step, I remember giving her a very wide berth, firstly to save my eardrums and secondly, in case she suddenly kicked out with the poisoned blades in her shoes.

In the late 90s, the average life expectancy of a Russian male was 58, well below that of most western countries and it's not difficult to see why. Almost all men smoked heavily, drank plenty of cheap vodka, ate little fresh fruit and vegetables and did hardly any exercise. I learned quite soon that, to do business there, you have to be firm, stick to your guns in negotiation and be ready to walk away if they try to grind the price into the floor. It's a game Russians like to play and they're very good at it.

When you begin to learn a little of their history, the reason for their hard approach to life becomes apparent. In the Second World War, the Siege of Leningrad (now Saint-Petersburg) alone, resulted in the deaths of up to 1,500,000 people. Many more were evacuated and perished in the cold or of starvation. The hardship lasted on through the Communist years and, whereas some of the older citizens still miss those times, most of the younger people are optimistic and outward-looking.

Nowadays, it's a thriving city with wonderful historic buildings and is home to the Hermitage, one of the largest art museums in the world. Things have really changed since Soviet times and there is now a wide choice of excellent restaurants, shops full of consumer goods and streets buzzing with expensive cars. I much preferred visiting Saint-Petersburg to Moscow. Moscow is far too big, sprawling over a huge area, it is home to over 12.5 million people and ranks very high in the world stakes of resident billionaires and air pollution.

I agreed with most customers that payment would be made to us in euros rather than roubles and that they would pay by direct bank transfer to our account. Generally, this worked well, even though these payments would sometimes mysteriously appear from strange accounts in offshore territories like Belize or the Turks and Caicos Islands. Others however, insisted on making payment in cash and some even insisted on using roubles. Rather than bring roubles back to the UK, we would change them into euros at a specialist exchange.

I remember Masha taking me to one such place, a highly secure building in Saint-Petersburg, where there were steel doors guarded by grim men in black combat gear armed with assault rifles and side-arms. Once inside, there were cubicles where one had to present identification and the roubles would be exchanged for brand new crisp euro notes. Masha told me that, just prior to one of my visits, two of the guards had shot each other out in the street. It wasn't a place I enjoyed visiting but the exchange rate was pretty good. I still sometimes wonder whether those crisp new notes were being printed in a murky back room of that building.

The journey between the two cities may be undertaken by air or by a fast train known as the Sapsan (it means the Falcon) which takes three or four hours to cover the 650 kms. The first time I made the trip though, trying to save money as usual, I took the slow sleeper train. This takes between eight and ten hours and I swear it runs on square wheels, judging by the bumps and rattles. I found myself sharing a two-berth compartment with a middle-aged Russian man who wore a huge grey bushy beard and spoke no English. He snored louder than anyone I've ever heard (and, believe me, I've heard plenty of snorers) for the entire night. I slept not a wink and arrived at my destination completely washed out.

One thing about travelling alone, it means you become accustomed to eating in restaurants alone. I generally take a book and, even if I'm just people-watching, I can at least pretend to be reading whist waiting for my food. Deciphering Russian menus can be interesting when there is no English version available. I remember seeing bear on menus, as well as elk, reindeer and odd species of fish. Where they do supply an English version, it's not always an advantage. I quote from the menu in one hotel, proudly offering:

'Tender Boiled Chicken Harts and Stomachs of Cream Filling'
'Beef Stake with Mush Potato'

or

'Hot Snakes'
'Vole in Truffle Sauce'

For me, one of the great perks of travelling is noting interesting translations of signs and instructions. In one German hotel, I stood waiting for the lift and read, 'PLEASE DO NOT USE THE ELEVATOR IN CASE OF FIRE' - so I took the stairs.

Still, we're not immune from signage blunders in the U.K. even in what is meant to be our native tongue. A friend recently sent me a photograph of a sign outside Northampton General Hospital, which reads,

Family Planning Advice
Use Rear Entrance

It's a fact of life that, in the textile industry, many businesses are owned and run by women. Russian women have a reputation for being more than a little ostentatious in the way they present themselves. In the Communist years, women struggled to feed and clothe themselves and their families. Life was really tough and now, when they do have disposable income, they like to spend it and flaunt it. There is a real hunger for the latest fashions and the younger Russians, male and female, are very much in tune with western styles. Sadly, the older ones are less successful. Whilst the men shuffle around wearing cheap shoes and garbed in ill-fitting dingy browns and greys, many of the women are all gung-ho for polyester and PVC, big jewellery and anything garishly bright and sparkly.

Some of the companies I visited were based in horrendous crumbling Soviet-era buildings with uneven concrete stairs and cast-iron pipes everywhere. Entering many of these buildings, you had to show identification to a surly uniformed guard manning a steel turnstile. I can only assume turnstiles were originally installed to restrict the crush of eager workers desperate to do their bit for the Motherland. There would be former rocket factories, now given over to small businesses, set in dismal, smoking, 'Mad Max' landscapes.

Surprisingly, through the rusting steel doors, there would sometimes be ultra-modern offices and work areas – all stainless steel and glass. There would be young women, looking as if they had just strutted off a Paris cat-walk, smart, sexy, well-educated and very keen to make it big in the world of fashion. I was often impressed by the drive and enthusiasm of younger Russians. I still believe that, if only the politicians there focussed on the economy rather than wielding military power, theirs might well be the wealthiest country on earth.

I became comfortable with travelling alone and always seemed to manage to find my way around, even in difficult surroundings. The Moscow underground system is a true wonder. Many of the stations feature marble pillars, ornate art deco lanterns, giant murals and bronze statues of heroes of the revolution. They are splendid palaces of transport, but I found it difficult to navigate my way around the system. All the signs use the Russian Cyrillic alphabet, on top of which, the station names are long and complicated. Here's an example: Красносельска - and that's one of the *shortest* names. I only survived by asking other passengers for directions in my very limited Russian. I always selected young people because they were the most likely to be able to speak some English.

In common with taxi drivers in many other countries, those in Russia are seemingly put on this earth to extract the most money from you in return for the least they can get away with. There are exceptions of course and I remember arriving at the railway station in Moscow late at night and, as usual, was besieged by a yelling horde of scruffy-looking cabbies. It was raining, I was dragging a heavy case and I weakened. Normally, I was used to fending them off but, this time, I was tired and I just didn't fancy tackling the metro. I haggled and agreed the price with a skinny, unshaven specimen, who grabbed one of my bags and ushered me, at a trot, to his car, which he had seemingly just retrieved from a scrap yard.

He jumped behind the wheel and proceeded to make showers of sparks as he hot-wired the engine into life. I assume it *was his* car, but there was no ignition key and he didn't need one. Before setting off into the mayhem that is Moscow traffic, he pulled out a huge thermos flask, poured two mugs of steaming black liquid and offered me one of them. I established that he was from Georgia and that the drink was Georgian tea – very famous. It was so sweet that I could feel my teeth dissolving, but I appreciated the thought. The remainders of my teeth were then shaken from their sockets as he drove like a man possessed. The car clearly had no suspension and, most of the time, the man's head was turned facing me in the back seat as he described the splendours of his native Georgia.

The hazards weren't limited to taxi cabs. I was once in Poland and had to travel from Łódź (pronounced Wudge), the seventy miles or so to Warsaw by train. I boarded an old-fashioned, compartment-type carriage with a narrow corridor and, as I tried to find my compartment, I was jostled by a man who seemed in a hurry to pass me. In fact, there were two men having some kind of altercation and then they were gone, chasing each other off the train. I thought it was odd behaviour and I instinctively felt inside my jacket. My wallet had gone and I hadn't felt a thing. My jacket had been buttoned up and I was wearing an overcoat and scarf but, somehow, cleverly, one of them had picked my pocket. I was encumbered by luggage but managed to reach a policeman standing on the platform. He ran off in the direction of their escape, but the two men were nowhere to be seen.

Apart from my British driving licence, there were only a few business cards and two or three credit cards in the wallet. I kept my cash, my phone and my passport all separately, so it could have been worse. As usual, it's the hassle of cancelling cards and so on that is annoying. The upshot of the incident was that I found myself in a noisy Warsaw police station making a statement. It was a dismal, crumbling building echoing with the sounds of hard-bitten officers dragging all kinds of riff-raff in and out of holding cells. I sat facing a bored-looking official behind a desk. He spoke a little English and he extracted a statement from me, sentence by laborious sentence and then typed it out in Polish, using only one index finger, on an ancient manual typewriter.

Of course, our business was as much about buying as selling. In order to sell competitively, I had to buy competitively, so I was always searching for new sources of fabric. This also took me to countries outside the UK, especially Spain, Italy and Germany. Now and again, the farcical situation arose where

I would buy a consignment of fabrics in say Germany, ship it back to Nottingham for checking and sorting, only to re-sell it to another client in Germany, only a few miles from where it was bought. I remember, in the true spirit of keeping costs low and saving time, I used to travel to Spain and back in one day to buy fabric, rather than staying overnight in a hotel. The trip involved driving for two hours to Stansted Airport, flying to Barcelona, driving for 2 hours to the supplier and there selecting and buying fabrics. Add to that the return journey and it meant twenty hours or more without sleep.

One feature of driving in that part of Spain was that, at intervals, there would be solitary roadside prostitutes trying to attract passing drivers. Usually posing provocatively on a white plastic chair, sometimes under a colourful parasol for shade, it was clearly such hot work that they couldn't bear to wear many clothes - maybe just a thong, a hint of a bra and a pair of sunglasses. Years later, a friend who had a house on the coast nearby once asked me with a wry smile if I'd seen 'those nice ladies doing traffic surveys'? Apparently many of these girls are from Russia and Eastern Europe and they are sometimes to be seen on very remote stretches of road. I imagine it's a risky business and they must be putting their lives in danger every single day.

One night, back in the UK, driving back homeward along the A1(M) northwards after one of the Spanish trips, I realised with a shock that I had actually nodded off at the wheel. I just had to stop and take a rest and I decided that, never again, would I attempt to cram so much into a working day. I discussed it with Tony and we both agreed that we were getting a little too old for that kind of pressure. It had become habit to work to the limit, but it wasn't worth risking our health and lives for, so we both began to use hotels a little more often.

We also began to use temporary workers to help out when there was too much heavy work for both of us to sensibly manage. These temporary workers were recruited through an agency and, over time, we used them more and more. One young man really impressed us because he showed a genuine interest in what we were doing, as well as being a good honest hard worker. His name was Emmanuel and he had been born in Ghana, but his family had migrated to the UK when he was a child. We decided that we would like to offer him a full-time job. He was happy to join us and he quickly became an invaluable member of our little team.

The world was shaken to its core on September the 11th 2001. I remember hearing the news for the first time on the little radio in my office. Al-Qaeda terrorists had crashed American Airlines and United Airlines planes into the twin towers of the World Trade Center in New York and another into The Pentagon. The death toll was almost three thousand and there were over 25,000 injured. This event triggered the so-called 'War on Terror' and the U.S. invasion of Afghanistan which had huge implications for the world. Security at airports was stepped up and the whole of humanity still lives with the aftermath of that shameful attack.

Twenty-Three

Clocking Off

Whenever possible, I continued to meet up with my old Nottingham friends each Wednesday evening. Attendances varied between two or three stalwarts up to a dozen or more and we gathered at a local pub, either in Nottingham or, more usually, one of the surrounding villages. Little had changed. We just enjoyed a simple meal washed down by good beer and the usual chatter about anything and everything. We would argue, tell silly jokes, reminisce and generally wallow in our combined friendship. We were all so comfortable in each other's company that, even if one went away for a year, returning to the gang was like putting on a comfortable old pair of jeans.

The nightlife of Nottingham was becoming less interesting to us as we grew older, but I still went into the city meet Gordon, Graham and JG sometimes for an early Friday evening drink. It was on one of these visits in 2004 that I met Paula, a university lecturer with a lovely lilting Welsh accent. I was fifty-three years old and she was twelve years younger than me. No sooner had we met than she disappeared off to Wales and I assumed she wasn't interested. In fact, she had rushed off to nurse her mother, who was dying of motor neurone disease, or MND. I can't imagine anything worse than seeing someone you love being taken by that awful disease and, sadly, within a few months, her mother lost the battle.

When Paula returned to Nottingham, we began dating. She was a single mother, working full-time and bringing up two young, mixed race sons. This was a new experience for me. I had once dated a divorcee with a young daughter many years before but, that aside, I was pretty clueless where bringing up kids was concerned. In the beginning, it was awkward but, over time, we began to gel as a family unit. We would take the boys to play football for a local junior team on Saturday mornings and stand on the touch-line cheering them on.

We both led very busy working lives and I really don't know how she juggled her work with being a good mum. I helped as much as I could but, I too, had to keep working hard. We went for weekends away and on family holidays to Devon. We sometimes visited Paula's father and other family members in Wales and my mother in Waddington.

Then, in 2010, she told me, quite out of the blue, that she didn't want to see me again. She had met another man. I was completely shattered by this bombshell. Only a few weeks earlier she had written me a love note and I was the best person she'd ever known. We had been inseparable. Six years had passed and I have no idea where the time went. To this day, I am unable to make sense of what happened.

If humanity is divided into optimists and pessimists, I tend towards the former. Not that I'm permanently wearing rose-tinted spectacles and a chirpy expression. I'm not like the man who fell from a twelfth floor window and, as he passed the sixth floor, was heard to say, 'So far, so good.' But, when things go pear-shaped, my response is to try to do something positive rather than dwell on what has happened. Doing something – anything – in the face of adversity, is the only way to survive and stay sane.

Whilst I took this rejection badly, my outward response was to throw myself into work and life in general. My friends were there as always and I thanked my lucky stars that I had always kept those friendships alive. I also made sure to keep in touch with my mum. She was remarkable, always busy in the house and the garden, even whizzing round the lawns with a motor-mower until she was almost ninety years old. She had a routine, meeting her next-door neighbour every morning for coffee and, every Tuesday, she would catch a bus into Lincoln to go shopping. Most of the seats on the bus were taken up by old ladies just like her, with white 'permed' hair-dos. As a result, the bus drivers apparently called it 'The Cauliflower Run', which she found hilarious.

It was around this time that internet dating was just beginning to take off so, with nothing to lose, I thought I would give it a try. I cheekily knocked ten years off my age, flatly refusing to believe that I was approaching sixty and wrote a glowing résumé. I attached the most flattering photograph I could find and waited for the offers to come flooding in….

After a disastrous first encounter with a lady who simply wanted a replacement father for her four year old son, I arranged to meet date number two, Karen, at a local garden centre. There, in the coffee shop, we nervously introduced ourselves and began to swap stories. I was fifty-nine years old but, in my vanity, had lied about my age to try to attract a younger model. I nervously spilled the beans about the age deception and was relieved that she didn't immediately storm off, quoting the Trades Description Act.

I found her attractive and instantly felt comfortable with her. I guess it must have been mutual because, against all the rules of common sense, on that first date, I ended up meeting her mother and joining in a quiz at her local village pub. We had so much in common. Our fathers had passed away, but our mothers were living. We each had a brother and a sister, nieces and nephews, but no children of our own. We had a shared love of the countryside whilst working hard in city-based careers. Karen worked for a large pharmaceutical company and spent hours each week driving between Lincolnshire and Cambridge. Whilst I lived in Wilford, a village on the edge of Nottingham, she lived in Denton, a small village in south Lincolnshire. I soon realised that I loved Karen and wanted to be with her for the rest of my life. It just felt right and she made me feel loved and valued, so I sold my house and moved in with her to make a life together.

Denton sits in the beautiful Vale of Belvoir, (pronounced Beaver), which straddles the border between the three counties of Lincolnshire, Nottinghamshire and Leicestershire. It's a pretty landscape of rolling hills, forged by farming and surrounding the magnificent Belvoir Castle and its estate. The quiet lanes and tracks are perfect for walking and cycling and there is a nearby reservoir and canal popular with anglers. The old village itself is home to only about two hundred and fifty residents and the old stone buildings are centred round the lovely 12th century church and the small school.

Not only did I have a new home, but also a new family because Karen's mother, Maudie, lived in a small cottage in the garden, with her poodle, Daisy. The other important members of the household were Meg and Jack, two happy, spoilt black Labradors. It was a great arrangement because, whilst Karen and I were out working, Maudie looked after the dogs and took care of washing, ironing and even putting hot meals on the table for us when we came home tired and hungry. She actually *enjoyed* washing and ironing and was never happier than stringing out lines of freshly washed clothes to dry. With a soft Irish lilt to her voice and a wicked sense of humour, she always played down the fact that she had health problems and had survived a heart-attack or two.

It was a busy life but Karen found time to be a member of the church bell-ringing band and, by way of a contribution to village life, I volunteered to wind the church clock. The clock machinery is housed in the ancient bell tower and is linked to the east-facing clock face, under which a tiny oak door gives access onto the main roof. Every week I had to climb the narrow stone spiral staircase, festooned with cobwebs, to access the tower. There I would wind, first the clock mechanism and then the striking mechanism, taking care not to over-wind them. It was surprisingly heavy work. I would also check and adjust any time discrepancies. It took a little getting used to and, in the early days, I confess to, once or twice, causing the clock to strike thirteen and there were other odd stray 'bongs' from time to time echoing around the village as I got to know the quirky machinery. The clock had to be wound several times a week and so I shared the rota with three other village men, Graham, Patrick and Ged. Sometimes, I would open the small door overlooking the roof over the nave and I would just sit for a few minutes to take in the expansive view of the village. It was so peaceful, high above the churchyard, looking eastwards over the rooftops and to the woods and hills beyond.

I hadn't been in the village for long when, sadly, Meg, the older Labrador, died and so we were left with just Jack and Daisy, the poodle, to keep us amused on our rambles. There came a time when Daisy was very ill and had to have life-saving treatment. We were desperate that she should survive because Maudie was devoted to her. Fortunately, the little dog made it, but was left with a certain wheeziness and a loud snore when she slept. So she was given the nickname, 'The Snuffle-Pig'. The Labrador, Jack was a lovely, gentle creature who liked nothing better than galloping around the fields and jumping in the canal at every opportunity, so he was known as 'The Swamp Donkey'.

Eventually, his health began to fail badly and, despite months of treatment, we had to say goodbye to him on Christmas Eve 2015. He was always terrified of visiting the vet, so much so that his teeth would chatter loudly in the waiting room. When the dreaded time came, we took him in the back of our estate car and the young female vet who had come to know him well, volunteered to administer the fatal dose in the car park, rather than put him through the stress of going into the building. It poured with rain. Karen cradled him and we were all crying our eyes out, including the vet, as the fatal dose was given and he peacefully passed away.

All this turned our thoughts more and more towards retirement. We began to realise that we were spending too much time working and, especially for Karen, job-satisfaction was in short supply. Both of us were travelling, spending time in hotels and driving from A to B for meetings and were getting tired of it. Karen was still commuting to Cambridge and flying off to America, South Korea, Japan and so on, doing a high-pressure job. I was slogging into Nottingham most days and then flying off to various European countries and Russia. We realised that we could afford to call it a day and decided to do it simultaneously. And so, in 2016, we each handed in one year's notice to give everyone concerned plenty of time to make necessary arrangements. I did a deal with my partner Tony, whereby he bought out my half of the business in timed installments. It was a great deal for him and it allowed me to make a smooth exit, so we were both happy. Karen and I both retired in spring 2017.

Twenty-Four

Heading South

At first I felt confused and a little guilty. Why wasn't I jumping out of bed at five or six every morning? After just a few days, I had to remind myself what day of the week it was. There were no deadlines, phone calls, meetings, deliveries or collections. I still dreamed about work and couldn't quite believe I was no longer part of it. I had spent a year preparing for this and, in the last couple of months had been informing all my business contacts about my departure. Some were envious and wished me luck and others said, 'Oh, I would die of boredom. I wouldn't know what to do with myself.' Thankfully, that was never a problem for me and I quickly discovered that time simply flew by. I swore to myself that, whatever happened, I would never fall into the habit of watching daytime T.V. That really would be the beginning of the end.

We kept ourselves busy but also began to relax and enjoy our surroundings. Karen loved having time to cook and would lose herself for hours, tending the garden. I exercised by chopping logs to store for our winter fires. We walked and cycled, often stopping at village pubs for lunch. I played tennis every week with my brother, Fred and a few friends and I still met up with the Wednesday night crew as often as possible. Karen and I began to treat ourselves to holidays in villas here and there. We had both spent years staying in hotels whilst working and we just loved the freedom of a private villa. No set times for breakfast or chamber maids knocking at the door. Flopping into a pool to cool off in peace and quiet and pleasing ourselves whether we took three hours over lunch, often just a home-made salad washed down with ice-cold rosé.

Over a few years, we rented villas in the north-east of Corfu, near Kassiopi, in Paxos high above the port of Gaios where I had sailed many years before and in Ibiza, near Cala Llonga on the east coast. One of our favourite areas was the northern part of the Costa Brava, in Catalonia, around the coastal settlements of Tamariu and Llafranc. We explored our surroundings, visiting local markets, losing ourselves in village backstreets and walking the coastal paths and hills.

Slowly, the idea began to form that we might buy a place of our own somewhere in the sun. There were pros and cons. The beauty of renting a villa is that you are not tied to one place. On the other hand, getting to really know a place is a joy and you are far more likely to meet local people and immerse yourself in their culture by living amongst them.

Many years before, my brother, Fred and his wife Sue, had bought a small fisherman's house in the lovely French port of Collioure, Catalonia. They spend as much of their spare time as possible there and I have visited many times. I love the place and I was intrigued to discover that one of my favourite authors, Patrick O'Brian, had lived there and is buried in the cemetery on the outskirts. He was a superb writer of sea novels and is renowned for his attention to detail and knowledge of the Royal Navy in the Napoleonic Wars. Probably the best known of his novels is 'Master and Commander'. He was a mysterious and secretive character who hid the truth about his background. It turns out that he had virtually no experience of sailing or the sea, but his writing on the subject is the very pinnacle of the genre. He is buried with his beloved wife and the grave is simply marked:

MARY O'BRIAN
1915-1998
PATRICK O'BRIAN
1914-2000

A few miles along the coast towards the Spanish border lies Banyuls-sur-Mer, a small resort and wine-producing centre. Every year, in October, the town holds a 'Fête de Vendages' to celebrate the end of the grape harvest. The idea is to reward the workers for all their hard work and each vineyard sets up trestle tables on the beach and builds pit-barbecues, using iron grids over the embers of old vine cuttings. At its height, there are three or four thousand people, feasting on roast wild boar, sardines and other treats, accompanied by gallons of the local deep red wine. The atmosphere is electric. Wild music is provided by a succession of raucous bands all dressed in colourful costumes.

We have made it an annual pilgrimage, under the guise of a walking holiday. We usually walk from Collioure across country and, as you turn the corner into the bay, it's quite a sight. Smoke from the many roasting pits rises into the hot sun and the noise of thousands of people having a high old time drifts across the bay mingling with the cacophony of the various bands. My favourite group was led by a character calling himself Mustapha Gonzalez. He was a slight figure, enveloped and dwarfed by a very battered old sousaphone. Dressed as a pantomime Mexican, all pink and turquoise, he was capped by an enormous sombrero with pom-poms. He put down a mesmeric deep bass beat with the sousaphone and the rest of the troupe, trombone, hand-held drums (bashed by a bull-fighter), saxophone and trumpet, joined in with flamboyant Latin anthems, belted out at full blast. Now and again, someone attached a ferocious fire-work to the sousaphone and the frenzy continued engulfed by sparks and smoke. I love it.

One of our favourite walks in the area is the climb up to La Tour Madeloc, a thirteenth century watchtower and beacon, about 670 metres above sea level. From the top, the 360 degree views of the mountains and the coast from are simply stunning. It's quite a hike and, if you're feeling really energetic, there's the option to continue along the peaks to a second tower, La Tour de la Massane. From there you are able to complete a circuit back down to Collioure, in total, a good 7½ hours hard walking.

Another enjoyable walk is from the Col de Banyuls, which lies 7 kms inland from Banyuls-sur-Mer. It's a mountain pass where there is a small refuge hut and views over the Spanish border. There are plaques dedicated to the 450,000 or so Spaniards who trekked over the border at this place to escape Franco's Forces during the Civil War. It was also an important escape route for fleeing Jews and Allied fighters in World War Two. Walking down to a secluded valley just over the border, there is a ruined monastery and a small restaurant serving massive steaks and welcome cold beers.

Fred and I found the crazy music of Banyuls so inspiring that we decided to have a go ourselves. He bought a trombone, Ray Smith bought a trumpet and I opted for a tenor saxophone, with the general aim of forming some sort of funky combo. I still enjoy playing saxophone, although progress is very slow. I'm able to knock out a few tunes and Fred has learned, much to his delight, that the trombone is a *very* loud instrument indeed. Learning any skill later in life is so much harder and I marvel when I think back to the heady days of the RAQ quartet when the music came fast and easy. The same applies to learning languages. I still speak reasonable French, learned so long ago at school but I now struggle with a few words of Spanish, forgetting as fast as I learn. As for Russian, only half a dozen basic words have remained in my thick skull. I suppose there was more incentive when in school in that failure to do homework meant being put in detention - or hit on the back of the head with a wooden blackboard cleaner.

For months after Jack died, Karen and I missed having a dog around the house and we had debated whether to have a new puppy. It's quite a commitment and, whilst we saw the drawbacks, we decided on balance that we wanted one. We reasoned that we would rather not have another Labrador for fear of constantly comparing it with Jack. The choices were narrowed down and eventually we decided on a Flat-Coated Retriever. They were popular game-keepers' dogs and gun-dogs in late Victorian times but Labradors slowly overtook them in popularity. They are renowned for their eagerness to please, gentleness, playfulness and sensitivity – and they look stunningly majestic. All these qualities appealed and we simply couldn't resist.

After an intensive search, we found a breeder in North Yorkshire who had excellent credentials. She was also a vet and had a fresh litter of black puppies for sale. In short, after a couple of visits to get to know the little chap, we found ourselves driving home with an eight-week old puppy who we named Harry. He was from a line of working dogs and show dogs and the breeders had made sure that, right from birth, he had been exposed to all kinds of sights and sounds to prepare him for life in the big wide world. Even so, he cried pitifully for the entire three-hour drive home. What had we done?

Once he was safely installed in his new home, Harry was fine. He was a tiny lump of fluffy black puppyness that turned our lives upside-down. We fell completely in love with him and, like doting parents, we devoted ourselves to his upbringing and future education. The first hurdle, however, was that he hated being in the car with a vengeance, maybe because he associated it with being taken from his mother and siblings. His crying was just heart-rending. We resolved it by making a great fuss of him whilst sitting nursing him in a stationary car with the doors open, then with the engine running, then moving a few yards on the driveway and so on, in tiny increments. It was a huge achievement when we managed to drive to the village church about five hundred metres away, without a whimper.

It wasn't long before Harry was so happy travelling in a car that, as soon as a door opened he would be in, as if to say, 'C'mon, quick, get a move on. Where are we going now?' In every other respect, the thorough preparation by his breeder had certainly paid off because, even as a tiny puppy, Harry was 'bomb-proof'. No sight or sound, however sudden or shocking, seemed to faze him. Police sirens, garbage trucks with clattering bins and flashing orange lights, thunder, lightning, fireworks, gunshots, jet aircraft and chainsaws - all were met with a quizzical tilt of the head and a wag of the tail. As time passed, he became an adored part of our family and, if ever we feel a little low, Harry, who is always happy, is guaranteed to cheer us up.

In October 2017, I was with my brother and a group of friends, staying in Collioure for a few days, when I had a telephone call in the early hours from Karen to tell me that her mother, Maudie had died suddenly during the night. Theirs was a very close relationship and Karen was distraught. I tried to get an early flight home but it just so happened that we were all delayed because of a French Air Traffic Controllers' strike and there was nothing I could do. The tragedy was that Karen had retired early partly to allow her to spend more time with her Mum. She had spent years working her heart out whilst Maudie held the fort at home. Now, just as mother and daughter were beginning to enjoy a little quality time together, the dream was cruelly shattered.

Within a year, my own mother, Betty, had also passed away. She was 93 years old and had been proudly independent until the last few months of her life. Although mentally still very sharp, she had begun to struggle with walking and then lost her appetite. She had always eaten so well, cooking fresh food as she always had and then, as if an off-switch had been thrown, she refused all meals. She became very weak, went to hospital and then into a care home. It was as though she had decided that she was tired and didn't want to go on any longer. We pleaded with her to take food but nothing and nobody could induce her to eat.

My sister, Susan, had been very close to her. They had shopped and been on holidays together, swapped recipes and garden produce. There's a special bond between some mothers and daughters that is unlike any other relationship.

Karen and I had always had plenty in common and now it seemed there was something more. We were now both without our parents and we grieved together. We had been blessed with loving parents for most of our lives and we had an awful lot to be thankful for, but suddenly we felt like orphans and we really would have to make our own way in the world.

Twenty-Five

Rear-View Mirror

Over the years I have learned a lot about my likes and dislikes. For instance, I'm no wine connoisseur, but I do know that I like a crisp Sauvignon and wouldn't thank you for a Chardonnay. I like to remain positive and objective, hopefully not turning into too much of a curmudgeonly old grouch. It's very easy to view the past through rose-tinted spectacles, ignoring all the wonders of being alive in the world today. I marvel at the benefits of today's mobile devices and the power of the internet, the reliability of modern cars, the variety of food in our shops and the opportunity to travel the world cheaply. It's hard to imagine, but my Dad never touched a mobile phone or saw satellite navigation and he only died in 1994. He used to talk about inventing some kind of roller-map on a screen to avoid wrestling with paper maps in cars. But of course, he thought in terms of mechanical solutions to problems and he had no inkling of the magic that was to come.

I have also come to the conclusion that many of life's real pleasures lie in simple things. For instance, when eating out, Karen and I nowadays often choose cheap and simple over pretentious and expensive. Firstly, we have eaten in hotels and restaurants all over the world; some good, some terrible.

Secondly, we like our own home cooking and so a meal out needs to at least be as tasty as our home-cooked food and also be served in a pleasing and relaxing atmosphere. There's no point in venturing out to eat overpriced rubbish, seated at a tiny table near the W.C., served by an offhand waiter who knows nothing about the menu.

We once booked a meal at the lovely Café Bleu in Newark. We wanted to treat ourselves after an especially tough patch at work and we had previously enjoyed very good meals there. The surroundings were provincial French shabby chic, muted jazzy background music, tasteful modern art and smiling waitresses. I forget what we chose for starters but, when it came to the main course, we both fancied the same dish; Beef Wellington. We were each presented with a plate on which there sat three discs of beef, no larger than fifty pence coins, three separate similar-sized discs of puff pastry and one smudge of brown paste. There were also three or four tiny Chantenay carrots that were completely tasteless and as hard as bullets. What the chef had done to achieve that level of hardness, I have no idea. I can only assume that he had previously trained as a blacksmith. The price of this dish was a hefty £22.50. We looked at each other in disbelief.

The smiley young waitress made the mistake of asking in her best sing-song voice, 'Is everything alright for you?'

'Since you ask,' I replied, 'Has there been some mistake? We asked for the Beef Wellington.'

'Yes?', she sighed quizzically.

'It's just that I was expecting fillet of beef wrapped in a crust.'

'Oh', she replied, 'This is actually Chef's *interpretation* of Beef Wellington – It's *de-constructed*.'

'Well', I replied, feeling a 'rant' coming on, 'Don't you think it would have been an idea to include *De-Constructed* on the menu so we might have had a clue? 'Chef' might also have included the word *Microscopic* in the description and, while you're at it, please tell him that the carrots are rock hard and tasteless.' Her expression changed to that of a bulldog sucking a wasp.

'It's a *very* popular choice, Sir.' Not long after that experience the restaurant went out of business.

A few months later, we were invited by friends to eat at an expensive Michelin-starred restaurant. On the menu was 'Lamb with Heritage Tomatoes and Burnt Tomato Ketchup'. The lamb was OK, as were the cherry tomatoes but, on the side, was a jet-black pool of goo. The goo had the taste and consistency of liquid charcoal. Needless to say, we have never returned. The sad thing is that some pubs in the UK are also jumping on the bandwagon and serving up dubious and pretentious food at silly prices. And whose bright idea was it to serve food on bits of wood or roof slates?

Of course, there is now far more choice out there and there are some terrific eating-out experiences to be had. I'm convinced that the greatest change during my lifetime has happened within *us*. Our expectations are higher and there is more choice than ever, so we have become more discerning. This doesn't only apply to the UK. Karen and I are spending more and more time in Southern Spain and one of the great delights is the 'Menu del Dia'. It's not difficult to find a superb three-course lunch for around ten euros. At 'La Pacomari' for instance, in the coastal town of Nerja, a leisurely lunch, seated in their shady courtyard is an absolute delight – and there's not a splodge of Burnt Tomato Ketchup in sight.

Somebody once said, 'Nostalgia isn't what it used to be.' but, whilst there are some real benefits of living in the modern world, it doesn't do any harm to remember the past and maybe question one or two changes. For instance, I love travelling by train and it does seem that governments are now at last waking up to the potential of rail transport. Sadly, the Beeching cuts of the 1960s saw the closure of about a third of the UK rail network and about half of the stations. The railways were haemorrhaging cash at an alarming rate and drastic action was needed. With hindsight however, many of those routes would be of tremendous value today in helping to reduce pollution, encouraging sustainability of rural communities and helping to ease road congestion.

It seems crazy to me that the UK imports fresh foods and other products from, say, the south of Spain, by road. Thousands of refrigerated trucks slog huge distances through the motorways of Europe, when trains would be far greener, faster and safer. It would need massive investment in regional hubs but the long-term benefits would be well worth it. The same applies to mail and parcel deliveries. Before 2004, mail was sent by train up and down the UK, being sorted overnight as it went. Maybe I'm missing something but, when the 'powers-that-be' decided to switch all of that on to the roads, was there any thought of the impact? I suppose these were the same 'powers-that-be' that had, in the late sixties, introduced the two-tier postage system to give them an excuse for failing to keep up the standard of a next-day delivery. It didn't go un-noticed by the baby-boomers, believe me. Still, I suppose we should be grateful that the cash raised by some of these measures was well-spent, propping up the generous pension schemes of state industries.

It's a fact that time seems to fly by more quickly as you age and, to a degree, it becomes more precious. I believe it was the great American comedian, George Burns who, having reached a ripe old age, was asked by an interviewer about his daily routine. He replied, 'I get up every morning and read the obituary column. If my name's not there, I eat breakfast.' I'm a big fan of George Burns, who died at the age of one hundred and had a terrific attitude to ageing. He once said, 'I was brought up to respect my elders, so now I don't have to respect anybody.' And, 'I love to sing and I love to drink scotch. Most people would rather hear me drink scotch.' Always positive, he said, 'I look to the future because that's where I'm going to spend the rest of my life.'

With that in mind, Karen and I began to realise that we were spending quite a lot of our time looking after our house and garden in Denton. Whilst we loved the place dearly, we didn't know what to do with what had been Maudie's little house and we liked the idea of making a fresh start. Somewhere with a smaller garden, easier to maintain, lock up and leave, whilst spending more time abroad. We loved the North Norfolk Coast and had been making our way there for short breaks, walking in the dunes and marshes. We had enjoyed the area so much that, in 2018, we had bought a holiday home there and were spending more and more time in it. We made a decision to sell our lovely cottage in The Vale of Belvoir and move to the Norfolk house permanently. The only down-side for me was the distance from my old friends in Nottingham, my tennis mates and my brother and sister. Karen would miss having a large garden to lose herself in but, on balance, we felt sure it was the right thing to do.

The Denton house sold quickly and, before we knew it, we were moving, lock, stock and barrel to our new home. Naturally, we were very sad to leave the village and our neighbours. We would miss the striking of the old church clock, the parkland with its huge horse chestnut trees and the surrounding countryside. Most of all, we would miss Mr. Mitchell, the retired farmer who, with his late wife, Gill, had taken Karen under his wing when she first came there to live years before. He had recruited her into the bell-ringing band and would frequently turn up almost out of the blue to have a coffee with us. If we weren't around, he would pop in for a chat with Maudie. He would make himself useful, catching moles, burning rubbish and keeping us up to date with news of seed drilling or how the harvest was progressing on his son's farm.

At the age of seventy, I look forward happily to what lies ahead. Although I look to the future, I can't help reminiscing about my past and the choices I made. Whilst out in the countryside, I'll occasionally catch sight of a forked stick or a white feather and I'll be momentarily transported back to a time with my Dad, fashioning a catapult or a flight for an arrow. I confess that, whilst walking with Karen, I have now and again, on a childish impulse, stuck sprigs of cleaver plant on her back or fired a 'plantain popper' at her, doubling the stem around itself to 'fire' the seed head, just as I used to do sixty years ago.

I still look forward to meeting my old friends, some of whom I have known for more than forty years. Too many others have sadly passed away, but those who remain persist in teasing, joking, arguing and sniggering as we always have done. We've all grown old without growing up and I wouldn't have it any other way. I enjoy meeting my brother for a game of tennis with Ray or David or Steve. We play hard to win but we're not competitive enough to dispute points or sulk if we lose. We pull faces or cough at the opposition to put them off. When I'm partnering Steve, he will say stupid things like, 'When I nod my head, hit it.' Usually, I'm with my brother Fred and, if he wants me to serve, he'll say, 'You go for it.'

I reply, 'Why are you calling me Hugo Ferret?' And so the madness continues. Then we all go to the pub for pints of Abbots Ale and bags of Nobby's Nuts.

When I see crowds of children flooding out of school, in their little cliques and with heads bent to their mobile phones, I can't help wondering about their hopes and fears. Their world is much wider and at the same time, more restricted, than the world I grew up in. Ageing is for old people, not for them –

and that's exactly as it should be. The spans of their lives will encompass changes and discoveries that are, for my generation, literally beyond belief.

Would I have changed anything about my life? Yes, certainly - all kinds of things - because, like any human, I've made plenty of mistakes. However, I am more than content to have lived when I did and do not envy those who follow. I have had freedoms unknown to them; freedom from social media, from mass communication and marketing and 24-hour T.V. When I was young, plastic packaging and bottles were unknown, glass bottles were re-used and sweets came in paper bags. Shops closed for half a day each week and always on Sundays. Whether or not you were religious, it provided a short period of respite and relief from the daily grind. Maybe it was a good thing – I'm not sure. If there's one thing I've learned however, it is that there is always something to learn.

Life has not been perfect but, on balance, it has been pretty good. I'm still an optimist, a day-dreamer and a dabbler and, after all is said, I still have absolutely no idea what I want to do when I grow up.